A Colorni-Hirschman International Institute 1

Critical Thinking in Action

Excerpts from Political Writings and Correspondence

Eugenio Colorni

Critical Thinking in Action

Excerpts from Political Writings and Correspondence

Edited by Luca Meldolesi and Nicoletta Stame
Translated from Italian by Michael Gilmartin

Bordighera Press

Library of Congress Control Number: 2019937319

Printed in the United States.

Published by
BORDIGHERA PRESS
John D. Calandra Italian American Institute
25 W. 43rd Street, 17th Floor
New York, NY 10036

A Colorni-Hirschman International Institute 1
ISBN 978–1–59954–145–7

TABLE OF CONTENTS

Part III

PREFACE

The name of Eugenio Colorni is quite familiar among the many intellectuals who knew Albert Hirschman. This is not true, however, of his work. The reason for this is that while Albert often spoke about his brother-in-law and close friend and acknowledged his influence on his own thinking, until now Eugenio's work, with one notable exception,1 has not been translated into English. Recently, however, "A Colorni-Hirschman International Institute" has begun publishing excerpts in English as part of a yearly dossier, "Long is the Journey. . . ," which is included on its website: www.colornihirschman.org. Building on this, Nicoletta Stame and I are now editing an initial sampling that reflects Eugenio's brilliance and ingenuity: a mini-anthology (which I hope will prove interesting and enjoyable) of texts taken mainly from a selection of Eugenio's political writings.

Born in Milan to an upper-middle class family of Jewish origin, Eugenio Colorni enjoyed a close-knit fabric of family and friends in the middle-class 'reseau,' the network that had sprung up spontaneously in central and northern Italy after the liberation of the Jews by the Risorgimento. He studied philosophy, and went to Berlin to learn from (and about) Leibniz, meeting Ursula and Albert Hirschmann[2] just before Hitler's ascent to power. He became professor of history and philosophy, first in a secondary school in Voghera and then in Trieste. He intensified his political activity, taking responsibility for the Internal Center of the Socialist Party, and was jailed by the fascist regime after racist laws were enacted by Mussolini in 1938.

He was then interned on the island of Ventotene, where, while developing his fascination with science and the philosophy of science,[3] he shaped the basis of the European Federalist Movement to-

---

[1]Colorni, "Prefazione" a Altiero Spinelli ad Ernesto Rossi, 1981; English transl. "Preface" to *The Manifesto of Ventotene*, by Altiero Spinelli and Ernesto Rossi 1981 (a blooklet that contains the "Ventotene Manifesto"); see below, III, 3.

[2]As is well known, landing in the US in 1940, Albert lost the final n of his last name.

[3] By working mainly on physics and with the legacy of Kant.

gether with Altiero Spinelli, Ernesto Rossi and Ursula Hirschmann.[4] Following his transfer to Melfi (Basilicata) for family reasons, he escaped confinement and reached Rome where, as a federalist and socialist, he helped lead a movement of rebellion that later contributed to bringing a victorious end to the creeping Italian civil war. Just a few days before the liberation of Rome, he was brutally gunned down while unarmed by the Nazi-fascists. He earned the gold medal for military honor of the Italian Republic.

1. The book is divided into three parts. The first focuses on Eugenio's early political writings (1935–37) and brings together texts that show Eugenio's largely spontaneous knack for finding existing loopholes and ad hoc solutions under difficult conditions — such as those produced by the strict fascist repression of democratic politics. I consider this group of writings a real discovery in political thought and action, and the source of a position later called "possibilism" by Albert Hirschman (1971).[5]

Indeed, an unusual feature of these brief texts is that they provide us with a lively and concrete introduction to Italian social conditions under fascism and to the inevitable conspiratorial dimension of the time. Led almost by the hand, the reader appreciates the feelings of the middle classes when faced with the war in Abyssinia (as an unintended effect of the fascist foreign policy), discovers the spontaneous communications networks that spring up among the people, and explores the function of the progressive teacher in the fascist secondary schools — a text which Eugenio intended as a model for similar pamphlets in various areas of political action.

This then is possibilism under conditions of political-social oppression and repression, and it is these conditions that lead the author to 'make a virtue of necessity' and develop the keen powers of observation and levels of practical engagement required in achieving the best possible outcome in the antifascist struggle. It is concrete necessity that sharpens the wit and produces small breakthroughs, enlightened proposals, ways around mental and material obstacles, etc.

---

[4]By discussing at length with this group, inter alia, the well-known *Manifesto* for which he later wrote the "Preface" in Rome (January 1944): see n1 above.
[5]Hirschman, 1971; Meldolesi, 2017, 2013 Ch. 2.

"Colorni, who was six year older than I," Albert Hirschman said,[6] "seemed ... to cultivate and relish an intellectual style that took nothing for granted except doubts. At the same time, he and his friends held fast to one certainty: they were firmly committed to opposing the fascist regime.

What was fascinating to me was that there was an intimate connection between the intellectual posture emphasizing an absence of firm ideological commitment, and the actual commitment to perilous political action. It was precisely the questioning and exploratory style with which Colorni and his friends were approaching philosophical, psychological, and social issues that impelled them to action in situations where freedom of thought was suppressed, or where they felt that injustice was obvious and stupidity intolerable. It was almost as though they set out to prove Hamlet wrong: they were intent on showing that doubt could motivate action instead of undermining and enervating it. Moreover, engagement in highly risky action was seen by them not at all as a price to be paid for the freedom of inquiry they were practicing; it was its natural, spontaneous, almost joyful counterpart.

Their attitude has always seemed admirable to me as a view of political action and as a way of conjoining the private and the public life. ..."

2. Except for a 1937 essay-letter (a little philosophical gem in itself on people and nature),[7] the second part of the book draws on Eugenio's 1938–42 writings from jail and internment and focuses on some concepts that he developed and articulated in those harsh conditions concerning such things as anthropomorphism, critical thinking, understanding, discovery, love etc.

To be more precise, Colorni, at the time overcoming depression and struggling against repressive mechanisms with possibilist ingenuity, was impressed by relativity and other scientific discoveries, and studied physics, biology, math and geometry, on top of philosophy, literature, psychology etc., with an emphasis on discov-

---

[6]Hirschman, Laurea Honoris Causa, Torino, November 12th, 1987; now in Hirschman, 1995, p. 118–19.
[7]"Our Image" (1937); see below, II, 1.

eries and innovations. He discussed politics with interned friends on Ventotene, and developed and/or refined ideas that turned out to be key advances.

Signs of this volcanic activity emerged here and there in the letters he wrote to Ursula Hirschmann and Silvia Colorni. Actually, the excerpts chosen reflect Eugenio's efforts to explain himself in simple terms, and his tendency to react kindly and sympathetically to obstacles and limitations. The excerpts herewith are entertaining as well as introductory, documenting Eugenio's interest in art and literature along with the natural and social sciences. They display the incredibly wide intellectual range in which he cultivated his passion for discoveries.

"The Project for a Journal of Scientific Methodology" that Eugenio sketched at Melfi (Spring 1942) shows his general position against anthropomorphism, a position around which many of his contributions can be assembled. Actually it is quite revealing of his intellectual maturity and clarity of intent, and the firm conviction that he had found his own way.[8]

Fragments on love selected from letters, essays and dialogues from this period represent both an important intellectual discovery and a bridge between his internment writings and his many later Roman activities in 1943–44.

3. The third part (1943–44) of the book draws on the final phase of Eugenio's persistent anti-fascist and anti-Nazi struggle. It presents a group of texts that point to some of the initiatives he undertook: not only as a socialist, journalist, and underground philosopher, but as a leading European federalist and teacher of young revolutionaries of the Roman resistance movement. Taken together they give us an idea of the insurrectionist strategy that Colorni then advocated.

Like Altiero Spinelli, Colorni had no idea of the dominant role the United States would play in the postwar period, but unlike Altiero, he expected a revolutionary movement in Germany that never came to pass. On the other hand, his key idea that the various peoples of Europe would be able to influence the contending victors in the conflict, and even to "prod" their decisions toward favoring a unit-

---

[8]Bobbio, 1975; Quaranta, 2011.

ed Europe is no simple feat of imagination. It is a groundbreaking notion that fits with what actually happened — of course with two considerations: that it is referred to events in the West, and that is extended over the postwar period.

"Unanimity" is the editorial of the second issue of *Unità Europea. Voce del Movimento Federalista Europeo [European Unity. The Voice of the European Federalist Movement]*, mostly written before the historic date of July 25th (the fall of Mussolini) and concluded afterwards by Eugenio Colorni, Guglielmo Usellini, Cerilo Spinelli (brother of Altiero) and others. Actually, the day after the fall of Mussolini, the Roman federalist group, the first in Italy to do so, flooded the city with leaflets calling on the people to rebel.

Guglielmo Usellini and Cerilo Spinelli were imprisoned, while Eugenio and others[9] succeeded in "putting to bed" and printing an underground edition of *Unità Europea*. In spite of popular rejoicing (fueled by hope that the war was at an end, which unfortunately proved illusory), Eugenio's editorial emphasized the difficulty of (and therefore the collective responsibility for) putting into practice the slogan unanimously supported by popular consensus: "Peace, out with the Nazis, liberty!"

On the other hand, like other federalists of the time, Colorni thought that postwar Europe would hold on to its traditional central role (economic, political and military). It is therefore likely that his possibilist conjectures led him to believe that the creation of a united Europe represented the advent of a great transformation: from a global nationalist-imperialist system to one that was federalist — based on brotherhood, freedom, social justice, etc.[10]

4. Moreover, in a a letter to Ernesto Rossi,[11] Eugenio anticipated issues — among them federalist politics as a movement and the eventual participation of federalists in party activity — that would

---

[9]According to the testimony of her son Daniele (see Rognoni Vercelli, 1991, p. 110, n. 35), Luisa Villani Usellini, while actively participating in the distribution of leaflets, was not identified.
[10]Until recently, this idea might have seemed outmoded. But the recent undeniable intensification of nationalist and imperialist rivalries has revived it. In view of these shocking (and dangerous) outcomes, shouldn't we make the effort to patiently reconnect with this Colornian thread?
[11]Now in Colorni, 2017, p. 179–82.

play a central role in the founding convention of the European Federalist Movement (Milan, August 28th-29th 1943), in which he played a leading role. But while Altiero Spinelli, Ernesto Rossi and Ursula Hirshmann went to Switzerland after the meeting to work toward the birth of a federalist movement in other European countries, Eugenio returned to Rome to put into practice his own daring political ideas.[12]

By September he was already in contact with the Socialist Party, and he began organizing groups of young people — first in the Jewish community and then among the socialists. He rejoined the Party, first becoming a local area military commander and then chief editor of the underground edition of *Avanti!* Aiming to promote a federalist movement within the Socialist Party, he wrote a statement of principles: "The Socialists and the European Federation."[13] Moreover, he edited the Roman edition of the Ventotene *Manifesto* (which later became the official document of the Federalist Movement) accompanying it with a highly instructive preface.[14]

Colorni took part in the rebirth of the Federation of Young Socialists, becoming their teacher and role model. Through this "special" relationship and other ones, Eugenio developed a threefold challenge which concerned the federalists of the Partito d'Azione [Action Party] (many of whom were content to settle for a propaganda campaign among the middle classes), the leadership of the Socialist Party (to urge the launching of a more combative, more incisive, more federalist political line[15]), and the Communist Party, with which he intended to compete for the leadership of the revolutionary movement.

---

[12]Holding fast to his strategic inspiration, Colorni puts his political initiative into practice in a way that goes well beyond what he had said in his letter to Ernesto Rossi on 5 August 1963 (see below excerpt III, 3); and, in his own way, gives us an exemplary theoretical and practical experience that is worth studying.

[13]See below, III, 2.

[14]See below, III, 3.

[15]As a socialist leader he was "a protester and a link," said Giuliano Vassalli, president emeritus of the Italian Constitutional Court (see Gui, 2010). A protester because he took the side of the young socialists who were champing at the bit concerning the party leadership, but also a link because his goal was to bring about a change in the ideas and behavior of that very leadership even while protecting the party itself. "I remember Angelo [Eugenio's pseudonym in the Roman resistance]," Vassalli reminisced (AA. VV., 2004, p. 40). "A great scientist, a great scholar, a great fighter for freedom, and at the same time a man who was splendidly political, exceptionally gifted at politics, propaganda and teaching — teaching us, that is, which was something that even though he was only a little older, he knew how to do."

In two articles of May 1944,[16] Colorni declared that the people have in their grasp the opportunity to bring about the advent of European unity[17]; while finally, in his "Tribute to Lopresti,"[18] he reminds us of the "flood of tears"[19] that even today is part and parcel of the genesis of a federalist perspective world-wide that might brighten future lives of women and men. . . .

I hope that this book will help provide an understanding of why and how "we all can still learn from Eugenio."[20]

Luca Meldolesi
A Colorni-Hirschman International Institute.
Rome, November 2018.

Crucial support for this book came from Eva Hirschmann Monteforte and Mario Quaranta. To them, our gratitude.

---

[16]See below, III, 4.

[17]The insistence on "change from below" in these articles by Eugenio (published in Rome by the underground *Avanti!* in May 1944) later ran into its ultimate "counterpart from above" in people like Albert Hirschman on the Marshall Plan or Altiero Spinelli on the European Commission and Parliament; not to mention Celso Furtado, Carlos Lleras Restrepo, Fernando Henrique Cardoso, etc.

[18]Eugenio wrote this "tribute" to Giuseppe Lopresti, martyr of the Fosse Ardeatine massacre, a few days before he was in turn murdered.

[19][di che lagrime grondi] Ugo Foscolo "Dei sepolcri" 1807, now in 1966.

[20]Hirschman, 1987, now in 1995, cit. p. 119.

PART I

1. Problems of War

This excerpt comes from the first full-fledged political article, signed as Agostini, by (a 26-year-old) Eugenio Colorni, on the fascist colonialist adventure represented by the Abyssinian war, which appeared in August 1935 in Politica Socialista[21] — *a journal published in Paris and edited by Angelo Tasca. In it, Eugenio spontaneously discovered his attraction for specific observations that would lead him to interesting openings and actions.*

We have criticized fascist foreign policy many times, but not always from the right point of view. The criticism has often been limited to noting and enumerating the "errors" of Mussolini's policies — their failures due to carelessness, a mania for theatrical gestures, and a wrongheaded notion of prestige — and to citing the setbacks suffered by Italy internationally as a result of such policies. . . . In the current situation it is senseless to criticize and pick apart every individual action, except as examples of a mentality and social organization that needs to be rebuilt from the ground up.

Actually, if we were to accept the basic foundation of Mussolini's foreign policy and evaluate its results on the generally accepted scale of diplomacy, it would be unjust and sectarian to seek to deny it a certain degree of skill and success. The contradictions it struggles with, the absurdities it faces and the abyss it will fall into are not the result of diplomatic mistakes or a lack of political clairvoyance. They are intrinsic to any policy that exploits national feeling (vibrant, essential, irrepressible and never to be ignored, but requiring other outlets and forms of expression) as an incentive for increasing the territorial and military power of one nation to the detriment of others.

In this regard, Mussolini has in a certain sense promoted the swelling of the boil which is now ready to burst. The tragic absurdity of Italy's present international position is a result of causes much

---

[21]Now in Colorni, 2017, p. 63–69.

deeper than a dictator's lust for greatness; it comes from the very essence of the interests he serves and the mindset he represents, which in one form or another now dominate Europe.

Indeed, it is clear that all the countries in Europe are struggling with the same absurdity that afflicts Italian politics. And this absurdity is the necessity of following a foreign policy line that is diametrically opposed to the line followed in domestic policy. After having promoted and assisted the rise of fascism in Germany, Austria and Hungary in every possible way and after briefly entertaining the possibility of a single fascist front against the democracies, Mussolini now finds that he is forced to ally himself with French democracy against a German fascism that has become intrusive. He finds himself forced in Austria to play off one fascism against another — this great upholder of national values stifling the most serious of the still unresolved national issues in Europe. He finds himself forced — and here the entire Italian press presents a ridiculous if not pitiful example — to conduct an anti-German campaign, professing shock at the very methods of propaganda and repression of which he was the original master, and creating the fable, unfortunately believed even by many of us, that there is an essential conceptual difference between fascism and national-socialism. Actually, one need only glance at the social makeup, economic ties, intellectual references, and tastes and styles of the two movements to be convinced of their essential similarity and to see that the most evident differences are due neither to their basic structure nor the goals they pursue, but to the natural differences, tendencies and emotional reactions of the two peoples. . . .

It is clear that our position must in any case be against the war, which this time will have a decidedly more imperialist character than last time, and that we must avoid falling into a union sacrée or anything similar. We will have to reinforce among the public the idea (already everyone's instinct, as clearly demonstrated by the initial reaction to the Abyssinian mobilization) that the war is in no way national in character, and is in fact nothing more than a last-gasp attempt to salvage fascism. The unpopularity in Italy of questions of foreign policy, the very fact that even today we don't know precisely with whom and against whom we must fight and that hate for one country and love for another will be imposed on us at the last minute — all these things will have to be taken into due account by us and turned to our advantage. At the same time, we must avoid any sort of general position of pacifism, or of passive resistance as conscientious objectors. We must not treat the war as an isolated phenomenon to be considered in and of itself. The war will be of a piece with fascism, its fatal and inevitable outcome, and it is as such that we must take it. We are not opposing the war as war, then, but rather opposing the fascist war and at the same time recognizing that this war can be a powerful step forward toward the end of fascism. We oppose the war, that is, from within the war itself. This will arm the Italian people; it will provide much more salient reasons for discontent than reduced wages or the abolition of freedom of assembly or of the press; it will give us the chance to let the masses see that their historic responsibility coincides with their own interests. It obligates us not to be absent or on the sidelines, but to be constantly present, active and close to the people, ready to guide their feelings and provide a goal for their confused aspirations; to make their active efforts concrete and productive. This is our task in the case of war if we want to act in accordance with our principles and in a way that will achieve something. The order of the day must not be pure and simple opposition to the war, but the transformation of war into revolution.

We must draw from this premise solutions for the concrete day-to-day issues that arise as the situation worsens. What I write here is not meant to do anything more than set out problems that will have to be painstakingly discussed. Already, the Abyssinia mobilization allows us to make interesting observations and offers new opportunities for our struggle. There is no point in deluding ourselves about the revolutionary possibilities that might derive from this enterprise, viewed in isolation. Even failures in Africa (which would be carefully hidden from the public and dressed up as victories) would not in my opinion lead to significant upheavals in this country. Meanwhile unemployment is creating a favorable situation for the government, leading to voluntary enlistments. In any case, these early reactions should be carefully studied as an indication of what may follow. First of all, there is a notable absence of enthusiasm, even among volunteers. Enlistment is an entirely calculated way of swapping their present unemployment for a job they hope will be lucrative and not very dangerous; they think that if the war were to become serious they would be called up anyway, and that until it is serious they have everything to gain and little to lose. They go to war in the spirit of mercenaries. I believe the strongest climate of opposition is to be found among the middle classes, where there is a feeling, more widespread now than ever and confirmed on this occasion, that they are at the mercy of a despotic will over which they have no control. For four days families watched their sons going off, in the wake of a simple postcard call-up, without knowing anything about their destination, without so much as a line in the newspapers. And suddenly there was a sense of panic; the muttering immediately began to get louder. Reassuring statements have quite naturally caused the anxiety to increase. Again, there is no need to overstate these phenomena, but perhaps on this occasion more than ever the Italian middle classes have the feeling that the chickens have come home to roost and that this fascism, for which they sold their souls as a guarantee against socialism, will bring ruin even to them.

Our movement will have to take these factors into account and not commit the traditional error of overlooking the middle classes. It should not be forgotten that without the support of at least part of this group, the revolution will not happen. If these classes should prove to be the starting point of an initial anti-authoritarian movement, we must not shut ourselves off from it, since it might be from there that our own anti-capitalist struggle begins. And this war, which for the first time does not affect the spiritual interests that the middle classes have shown themselves willing so casually to give up, but rather strikes at their closest material interests, may awaken in them some desire for autonomy and freedom. It is to them, therefore, that we must direct our propaganda, using language that responds to the state of mind described here.

Another problem, one of detail but important nonetheless, is the position each of us must take in response to the call to arms. I would like to propose a rapid discussion of this, since for some of us it is a tragically urgent issue.

The solution of leaving the country carries the implicit conviction that in the case of war all revolutionary action must fatally
cease and that the only reason to stay would be to save one's personal dignity. But it is precisely in the event of war that revolutionary action begins. War gives us an unprecedented opportunity for
contact with the masses, and with masses who are in a condition
particularly suited to accommodating revolutionary ideas. Disen-
gaging from them in this situation would be a serious mistake. We
must go to war, but as revolutionaries determined to sacrifice our
lives not for the cause of the war but for the cause of the revolution.
Our action will play out in barracks, trenches, and hospitals. How
will it happen? What are its methods, its organization? These are
the extremely important issues that I suggest should be debated.

Agostini

2. Spontaneity as a Form of Organization

This is a surprisingly innovative article (signed as Anselmi) by Eugenio, written with the upcoming Congress of the Socialist Party of June 1937 in Paris in mind and published in Nuovo Avanti! *on June 12th, 1937.[22] Contrary to prevailing doctrines, and based on the observation of the day-to-day life of workers and their families and friends, Eugenio asserts that spontaneity is itself a form of organization and that the party should adapt to the rhythms and propensities of the people and not the other way round.*

At the beginning of the year Mussolini's visit to Trieste was officially announced. On February 12th the Fascist Federation proclaimed imminent "the satisfaction of our ardent desire" and advised the public that they would be signaled without prior warning, by means of bells and sirens, to assemble immediately in the central square. Sometime later, following the signing of the Italo-Yugoslav pact, it was said that the Duce would surely come and speak words of reconciliation from this advanced outpost.

We have now reached the beginning of June, and of the Duce we have seen not a trace. Why? If you add the fact that since coming to power he has not once set foot in Trieste, and that years ago he mustered the courage to drop anchor aboard a warship in the port without coming ashore, the fact appears even stranger.

The Reason for a Missed Visit

There can be only one explanation, paradoxical as it is, given the vast means at the Duce's disposal: fear. He stays away because he knows that he would be badly received by the people, because he is afraid of an assassination attempt by Slav nationalists, and because he is angry with the bourgeoisie which, as he once put it, "don't understand fascism."

And who are we to say he is wrong? The fact is, the atmosphere

---

[22]Now in Colorni, 2017, p. 87–95.

of discontent with the economic situation and with political oppression, along with hatred of fascism, has progressively increased in the last few months. The Julian proletariat, composed of construction workers, Istrian miners, seafarers, stevedores, and above all of the unemployed, has an old revolutionary tradition that has never been discredited. Their position at the border, their contact with central Europe on one side and with the Mediterranean on the other, gives these people a background and sensitivity not easily found elsewhere. Their relatively high level of education allows them to read the economic and political truth between the lines of the newspapers and to reject the rubbish foisted on them by party officials.

I can say without exaggeration that the number of fascists among them does not amount to 1%. On the rare occasions when union leaders want to select their trustees from among the workers, they have trouble finding even one who is a party member; and if they find one it is still no guarantee that he is a fascist.

The masses, who this winter have seen the cost of living go up by 30%, no longer make the slightest secret of their discontent.

You would say that they feel a certain sense of impunity, that they are aware that if the police wanted to punish everyone who complained they would have to lock up the whole city. Interest in the affairs of Spain and France is huge. Radio broadcasts from Madrid and Barcelona and from underground Milan are followed with religious devotion. People are going into debt to buy radio receivers.

I would say that the battle being fought outside our borders has concentrated energies and restored everyone's sense of belonging to an immense working community; it has swept away the feeling of isolation that has been our main obstacle to action.

Antifascist Demonstrations

In April and May there were major antifascist demonstrations. In the Arsa mines they were awaiting the visit of the Duce to mark the opening of the recently constructed workers' village. Then one morning the walls were found covered with revolutionary and anti-fascist graffiti. The writing was removed and the entire shift that had worked that night was locked up. But the next morning the same graffiti had once again appeared.

The interior of the Barcola church was discovered one day to be covered in hammer and sickles, in red paint. The newspapers couldn't avoid reporting the fact, which had made a strong local impression, but they attributed it to a drunkard and replaced the hammer and sickle with . . . a heart with an arrow through it! Hammer and sickles were also found in the cemetery. On May 1st the red flag was flying at the San Marco shipyard. Similar stories arrive from every part of Italy.

Wage increases were greeted by the entire population with utter indifference. The papers had previously warned that these raises should not be considered a victory for the workers but as a gracious gift from above. But the fact that they arrived precisely on May 1st made it plain to everyone this was an offer made grudgingly by the government at a moment when they felt that the wave of discontent had risen too high.

And workers who on average earn 90 lire a week are not exactly inclined to feel that they have benefited much!

Such is the situation of the proletariat. But even the Triestine bourgeoisie, battered by the general crisis and by the particular postwar situation that afflicted Trieste, are liberal and Massonic, and have never been fascist.

Trieste is without doubt one of the cities in Italy where there is the most discontent, the most grumbling.

The Function of Revolutionary Parties

In an atmosphere so favorable to our struggle, what is the revolutionary parties' function? We have to admit that the work done has up to now been far from equal to the task imposed by the situation.

We can safely say that every worker in Trieste is a communist or a socialist, that every bourgeois Triestine is a liberal or a republican. We can also say that people who think in the same way meet and exchange ideas. Spontaneity is the characteristic feature of every demonstration. The organized parties, be they communist or socialist, which could easily accomplish something really worthwhile, maintain contacts with the masses that are still too sporadic. With respect to the masses, the parties have fallen behind. This was the dominant feeling we had on those days in April and May when the excitement — and not only in Trieste but all over Italy — started to reach impressive levels.

It is too easy to blame the relative ineffectiveness of the parties on human shortcomings. It probably originates in certain structural defects that prevent them from controlling and taking full advantage of the moods that arise spontaneously among the masses.

The popular movements of recent months, the influence of the events in Spain, and the enormous success of the radio broadcasts suggest certain considerations that we present as an attempt to adapt to a concrete experience in a specific situation.

Our revolutionary parties started out with the premise of forming an organization that would allow the center to reach the base, each party operating through one responsible element or more who would be in contact with the higher authorities. Recently, in recognition of the disadvantages of a pyramidal hierarchy, an attempt was made, particularly by the communist party, to eliminate all connections between groups, and to keep each group connected directly with the center by means of a "circulating" trustee.

It is also clear that in the tactics for penetrating the fascist trade unions each group needs to be directed and guided in this action by a party representative who is an essential part of the group.

The Problems with a Certain Type of Organization

It is almost pointless for me to dwell on the enormous difficulties that make this kind of organization a labor of Sisyphus. First of all, it comes up against the difficulty of finding men at the base. Looking for direct collaborators in every workshop, every trade union, every neighborhood, is much more difficult than might be imagined, considering the general mood among the masses. The socialist or communist worker, although extremely concerned with political problems, is today reluctant to take on specific responsibilities which he knows carry great risks and whose effects long experience has made him skeptical about. Cadres formed in this way have always been unstable, deficient and inconsistent. The form of organization consisting of groups linked to a single trustee would be excellent if such groups were already there, formed and organized and ready to make contact with the center. But if they are not? The job of forming them cannot be done by a single trust-ee; this would entail a set of relationships and ties of a type that can wreck a group even before it begins working.

Experience teaches us that the greatest dangers arrive when individuals from different environments come into contact: in-tellectuals and workers, trustees from the center and individuals from the base, petty bourgeois and proletarians.

People with different mindsets and different habits end up hav-ing trouble understanding each other, losing their political sensitivity and no longer able, in an environment that is not theirs, to recognize provocateurs and spies. Obviously, the difficulties listed here are typ-ically part and parcel of our work, which we know is not easy — and I would not dream of proposing that we abandon our deeper efforts which, though continually interrupted by circumstances, must be steadfastly renewed. That said, however, I would like to suggest the possibility of a type of work which, although less radical, would be more wide-ranging, a type whose true scope and possible develop-ments were revealed in the anti-fascist wave of last April.

Spontaneous Action and Organizational Action

Our political parties' behavior toward the masses has always been based on the idea of having to organize them in keeping with the parties' own structures and methods. Spontaneity has always been considered a sign of both the maturity of the masses and the weakness of the party. "Spontaneous" action and "organized" ac-tion have always been set in opposition like two antitheses. Too little thought, however, has been given to the idea that in every mass political action there is an element of organization, perhaps difficult to pin down, which is very important for us to understand if it is to serve our purposes. We commonly refer to any action as spontaneous if it hasn't been directed by a party. It hasn't occurred to us that spontaneity is itself a form of organization. (It goes with-out saying that this has nothing whatever to do with the reform-ist and trade unionist spontaneity that Lenin was addressing in "What is to be done?," but rather the spontaneity in the revolution-ary momentum of the proletariat).

The immediacy of people's reaction to recent events and the

speed at which news, moods and slogans spread have revealed elementary forms of organization latent in the masses that it would be a very serious mistake to ignore.

Connections — person to person and group to group contacts — exist independently of parties. They are the links of long-standing friendship, kinship or cooperation that every worker has with every other, they are the ties of shared labor, reciprocal trust and everyday habit. The spirit of the masses is so homogeneous and widespread that every worker and every bourgeois may be said to have his or her own way of obtaining information, expressing opinions, commenting on facts; they each have, in other words, a personal political environment that feels safe, and that they wouldn't want to trade for other regulated and tested systems. Up to now, these environments have almost always been reserved for ineffectual grumbling and harmless gossip. But they can quite easily (as we have seen in recent months) evolve into more serious shapes. Once a word, a news item, or a pamphlet has been inserted into this network, it moves and spreads by itself, with no need for an additional push, and in no time it is a word or pamphlet that is known to everyone.

The Propaganda Significance of the War in Spain

This situation, it seems to me, makes our work immeasurably easier.

The socialist or communist worker feels no need to make new contacts. He is not isolated at all. What is missing is not a sense of solidarity in the workshop, at home or in the tavern but rather a wider sense of solidarity that extends to the nation and the whole working class.

What is missing is the sense that the ideas that he and his friends develop are not just relics from the past, but are ideals that the affairs of the world still revolve around. This is the propaganda value of the war in Spain. Today once again the workers know that they are part of a whole; they have recovered their center of gravity, the security of being in the right, their trust in the future.

The party's job will be to make use of this system of natural connections, invisible to the police, and give it political fuel. This does not mean eliminating spontaneity, but rather cultivating it, strengthening it, giving it content. Between the so-called uncontrolled action of the masses and the totally steered and disciplined action of the party there is a scale of infinite gradations. And concrete political action will from time to time graft itself to some point on this scale.

The April movements were spontaneous, it is true, but it must also be said that they were encouraged, thanks to the deeds of our comrades in Guadalajara and Bormeo and to the rapidity with which these victories were brought to the attention of the masses. We must act on this spontaneity among the masses, giving them increasingly precise directives and increasingly concrete words.

But if we want to avoid the dangers I have mentioned, we have to do this impersonally, allowing the latent and secure system of connections operating at the base to function as a distribution apparatus.

Among the means available for this purpose, the recently rather neglected press has a predominant role to play. The main risk of newspapers as a propaganda vehicle is the difficulty of their distribution, which can easily allow the police to piece together the structure of the organization. But when distribution is entrusted to a system that is automatic, so to speak, and separate from the organs of the party, the only problem left is delivery and packaging at the site. This is not a serious difficulty and resolving it only requires a very small number of secure officers. The danger is greatly reduced both for readers and distributors (who would be friends, relatives, longtime acquaintances). Contact between center and periphery is no less direct and immediate this way than it would be if there were a cumbersome and dangerous network of emissaries and trustees.

The Importance of the Illegal Press

And the press can closely follow not only national and international events but also actual daily life among the masses without identifying leaders and managers.

It can follow and direct and promote the work of infiltrating the unions and fascist organizations, which we regard as possible and productive but to which (it must be said) the masses have thus far been unresponsive. This will also greatly ease the work of the few at the top, who would be freed from direct political contact with many elements at the base, a type of contact through which agents provocateurs are known to be easily inserted. The leaders will then be more free to pursue their connections with foreign comrades and their press work, responsibilities involving narrower technical expertise and a number of managers that is limited and not easily known. They will of course need to maintain contact with the masses to keep abreast of their needs and moods and follow their movements. But they can do this innocuously, legally, without betraying their illegal activities. Other means in addition to the press could also be devised. The radio is a very powerful example. But for these tools to be truly effective, the important thing is that their use should be regular and frequent, and they must be rich in political content and information. We do not want generic leaflets and simple phrases. We want to do a real job of education.

I do not mean to say that this would solve all our problems. But I do maintain that at a moment when any form of organization will run into enormous difficulties, this way is perhaps the simplest, the one that will save the most energy. It is easier to throw the birdseed so that the pigeons come and get it on their own than to feed it to them one seed at a time.

And this also means mounting an appeal, a call to our comrades across the border. Promote the copious, regular and frequent entry of printed news; look after the radio, organize general channels of propaganda. Furnish as much news as is possible. We, for our part, will also do our best in this direction. Let us make use of the vehicles offered by the enormous discontent reigning in Italy today.

Anselmi

3. The Function of the Teacher in Fascist Schools

As a secondary school teacher Eugenio carefully studied the reactions of the students, writing these illuminating articles (which appeared in Nuovo Avanti!, July 1937,[23] with the signature Agostini) based on his observations. Refusing to countenance any sort of apologia, they serve as a guide for teachers of middle-class students under authoritarian conditions, particularly with regard to explaining fascism objectively in a history course. Colorni felt that these articles, printed as a pamphlet, might also serve as an example for analogous elaborations in other sectors.

Middle-class Students

The problem of the political education of young people has quite different characteristics in elementary school, secondary school and at the universities. In primary schools it is mainly a problem of training the class of teachers and educating pupils' families through the teacher; that is, the problem primarily concerns the contact between the petty bourgeois teachers and the proletariat that the vast majority of pupils belongs to. In the universities, the work must take place in student circles directly, not only in the classrooms. Middle school, on the other hand, offers the possibility of direct influence of professors on students during the lessons, and presents a class of teachers that is particularly qualified for such work.

And first of all it should be kept in mind that secondary school cannot be identified, as it too often is, exclusively with Classical High School. Secondary school not only produces university students and the future so-called ruling classes but also — and mainly — the totality of clerks, officers, teachers, shopkeepers, accountants, surveyors and technicians who make up the middle classes that have up to

---

[23]Now in Colorni, 2017, p. 97–109.

now far too easily fallen prey to fascism. The families of the students generally belong to these same classes and often (especially in the case of technical schools, teacher's colleges, and industrial and commercial institutes) to the upper layers of the proletariat. These classes aim to move up, to improve their social position, and therefore to be responsive to the appeal of fascist bourgeois ideologies in which they recognize the ideals of the classes they aspire to belong to; but it would be a most serious mistake to abandon them to their fate based on this bourgeois lackey tendency. In the secondary schools the young people who belong to these classes comprise the highest percentage of good students. They are attentive, intelligent, and interested in their studies, and school is for them not a burdensome obligation but rather a tool for success, an investment of time and money from which they seek to reap the maximum possible benefit. They often make sacrifices in pursuit of this aim, even against the will of their parents, who would like to see them working and earning as soon as possible. The fact that in many schools around a third of the students are partially or totally exempt from fees on the basis of merit gives an indication of the force of will of these young members of the petty bourgeoisie, the agricultural middle class and the proletariat, who see in education their only chance to rise from the poverty of their present state.

Now these young people's earnestness and sense of responsibility opens them to a curiosity about life that makes their political education easy and productive. Having been raised in a climate of fascism and almost unaware of the possibility of any other conception of politics, they are nevertheless eager to find some content in the empty words of propaganda they hear from the O.B. (Opera Nazionale Balilla: a fascist youth organization) hierarchs. It is true that they have no wish to object; but they do have a great desire to explore. In a confused way they hear in political problems a concrete expression of collective morality; they have a sense that this is where their most important material, moral, and intellectual interests are decided; they are bored and disaffected by simple phrases.

Professors have indisputable moral influence on them. Unlike students from rich families, who see in their teacher little more than some poor devil paid to give them lessons, and who are constantly led into a contemptuous comparison between the teacher's modest standard of living and their own luxurious lives, the great majority of students see the professor as the most cultivated person they ever come into contact with, and sometimes also (depending on the professor) the one with the broadest views.

He has travelled, he has a university education, he knows some foreign languages, he has had contact with the upper middle class. In their eyes he often represents the man who has achieved the modest ideal of bourgeois esteem that they aspire to. If the professor knows how to make use of his daily contact with his pupils so that one way or another he takes part in the things that interest them, if he is able to establish a certain confidence with them, and especially if he allows them the freedom of speech and discussion in the classroom which makes the lessons lively and interesting, if he is careful to free himself of all the musty scholastic and doctrinal rot and to come before his students as a modern man, living in his own time and taking an interest in today's problems; then he will easily succeed at winning their hearts and will gain significant influence over them.

Now secondary school teachers are largely not fascists. Whether enrolled or not, they still belong to the intellectual bourgeoisie that finds its spiritual bread and butter and its intellectual and moral purpose in struggles and debates over democracy. The youngest of them belong to the group of somewhat peculiar youths who in departments of arts and sciences distanced themselves from the sporting and carefree lives of the fascist students. Dedicated fascists are rare among secondary school professors; many have gone along, with or without difficulty, in a spirit of bureaucratic acquiescence; not a few of them still maintain an attitude of manly independence. Finding precise currents of political opposition among them would be difficult. Their opposition is generic, often of a liberal and masonic nature. It is the opposition of the intellectual offended in his most prized possession: his freedom of conscience, and exasperated by continuous mandatory interference in his teaching.

The teachers find themselves grappling with school curricula that at every turn impose statements and explanations of fascist concepts and ideals. This is highly embarrassing for them, and not only on the occasion of official commemorations, but in their actual teaching as well. Courses in Italian, history, Latin, philosophy, economics, and law constantly compel them to say things they don't believe and to glorify people and ideals that are hateful to them. This is precisely the issue that we think needs to be examined.

Almost all teachers under fascism are essentially concerned with protecting their dignity, adopting a severe and disdainful attitude, where possible avoiding gestures and words that show acquiescence or participation in official policy, and either passing over thorny subjects or addressing them with a tone that clearly shows that they do so under obligation and against their conscience. This more or less pronounced attitude is one of passive resistance; it has a certain nobility and is positive in the impression it can make on the students, which is that independent spirits and clear consciences do still exist; that there is still room in the world, and not only in books, for the attitudes of the heroes of the Risorgimento, for a Cato, a Bruno, a Vanini.

In this way the teacher has at least partly protected his conscience, his moral prestige. But has he looked after the education of his students? With this stance he has looked after his duty to himself, but not to the part of society he is professionally called upon to affect. One might respond that the example he sets is in itself educational. But what is the educational value of this mute example that dodges explanations? The students may or may not admire it, but they do not understand; and most of the time they consider the professor's reserve as simply the quirkiness of a man who belongs a world gone by.

To be satisfied, in front of young people, with this position as a "relic" or (as in some cases) to be almost pleased with it is not only sterile, it is reprehensible: it is surrendering and becoming an artifact commemorating one's own defeat.

The young are eager for explanations. They are impatient for those moments in the course when the professor is supposed to open up a bit, explain things, justify his attitude. And they are disappointed and irritated by the embarrassed and elusive phrases they get instead.

It is not true that students are in themselves inert and indifferent. They are when what they are offered is the usual declamatory fare; but as soon as they get into an actual political discussion they are more than interested.

Indeed, such discussions are the only conversations they are deeply interested in. And what's more, they don't know, they don't realize, that such discussions are prohibited. The great majority of young people today (especially the petty bourgeoisie) have never heard politics discussed, other than in a strictly local sense. They have never had occasion to experience the oppression of the police, because they have never known opposition, rebellion or struggle. They do not know in detail what a political party consists of or how a democratic state is organized. And it is precisely this ignorance, this intellectual segregation, that is fascism's most powerful weapon. It is more powerful than favorable enthusiasm which, being attentive, involved and active, can therefore quickly change to disappointment and rebellion.

Now this ignorance, what I would call almost political naiveté, leads young people to view with great curiosity any perspective that opens new horizons to them, and shows them flashes of other social possibilities; it is curiosity about what is new and different, untroubled by any suspicion that it has already been officially branded disgraceful and is punished as a crime. And so, if on one hand the fascist teacher's empty ranting bores them, on the other, the decent, shy and reticent tone of the anti-fascist teacher, unaccompanied by anything remotely positive, arouses their suspicion: what they usually sense is sterile obstinacy.

Now how is it possible to escape from this ivory tower and make the sort of contact with young people that responds to their needs? And at the same time, how is it possible to put into operation an anti-fascism that does not risk becoming an empty ceremony of abstention for personal satisfaction. The answer in what follows.

Discussing Fascism Objectively

Obviously we cannot propose that explicit antifascist propaganda should be disseminated in the schools. But I think the only possible solution is that instead of ducking them, the teacher should face up to current political problems, especially the question of fascism; that he should overcome his horror at things he would rather not mention, aiming to arrive at an objective account, especially from a historical standpoint. He should first of all make it clear to the students what fascism is: how it arose and what its historical and doctrinal origins are. Young people don't know these things and, despite the provisions of the curricula, they don't learn them from their fascist professors, who limit themselves to vague and inconclusive panegyrics. The antifascist professor can earn the respect and gratitude of his students if he explains to them in a way that is objective, historical and scientific what these things that they are expected to idolize really are and, even more importantly, what the things are that they are expected to revile. Left in total ignorance about these things — and this quite often happens during lessons in history or corporate law — the students have to ask the professor what liberalism or socialism or communism refers to.

Explaining these things clearly and pervasively is not only possible, it is the official duty of the schools. And when students know and understand them, this is already a formidable element of propaganda against fascism.

It is not at all necessary that the professor should take a position. All he has to do is explain objectively, just as he lays out the facts of history objectively and without bias. And the facts speak for themselves: young people, on their own, whether because of social background or material and moral interest, will be drawn to the ideas they feel most strongly connected to.

This form of influence and education cannot be prevented by any ministerial directive, not unless the ministry decides to eliminate fascism from its curricula. But every time someone speaks of fascism, any conscientious professor should not be able to avoid framing it historically, and showing its position with respect to other political views and to the international situation.

What will we get back from this? The young people in the schools will certainly not simply and immediately become antifascists. Suggesting this as a goal would be utopian and absurd. But what we will get is that an intelligent student will realize that fascism is not the only possible and existing political reality, nor salvation sent to us by God to fight all evils, nor the army of light struggling against the army of darkness; but rather that it is one of several political systems, that it protects certain interests and opposes others; that it is predominantly represented by certain social classes, follows certain traditions and repudiates others, and takes a specific position when it comes to certain internal policy methods, which are distinct from other methods. What these conceptions are, these interests, these methods, and those they oppose (not just that the former are good and the latter bad): this is what all young Italians, who were born and live under the fascist regime, want to know. This is what every conscientious teacher, fascist or not, has the duty to teach them. And simply learning such concepts is of inestimable value for our struggle and has a destructive value for fascism, which cannot be maintained without suppressing and disguising the truth.

Without wishing to give directives that are too detailed, I will indicate some examples of how instruction that adheres more closely to the needs and attitudes of the students might be practically implemented by teachers of any political shade, without incurring any danger of disciplinary or police action.

The word 'homeland' has so often been dragged through the mud of fascist propaganda (and for that matter by all reactionary propaganda), it has been so cynically used for supposedly righteous purposes, and it has with such deliberate skill been used to sell ideologies of selfishness, social oppression, and international plunder, that all socialists and antifascists now hesitate to pronounce the term for fear of being mistaken for those who speak the word only to prostitute it. It nevertheless remains a word that carries the evocation of a certain ideal and finds an immediate heartfelt response, especially among the middle classes. It is a word that young people have since their childhood been in the habit of pronouncing with devotion, as a symbol of everything pure and unselfish. Are we to allow this word to be stolen by the people's enemies?

The professor who to distinguish himself from his fascist colleagues does not speak of the homeland at school risks incurring the incomprehension and contempt of the students. He risks being seen as coldhearted in their eyes, closed to collective ideals.

But the word homeland has a value that goes much deeper than the way it is used by the class of exploiters to gain an advantage by confusing people's ideas.

Why not explain this value to the students? Why not teach

them that the feelings that go with the homeland are nothing else but the sense of belonging to a community that has its own particular characteristics with respect to language, culture, history, traditions, and political and social problems, along with the will to resolve these problems within this same community? And why not emphasize actively resolving them and the fact that loving your homeland means getting to know its evils, contradictions and internal injustices, and trying to change it?

In this way young people will acquire a concept of homeland that is different from the imperialist idea based on believing, obeying and fighting, but is not for that any less seductive, but rather is much more responsive to their need for responsibility and sacrifice. They will come to realize that we ourselves are the homeland and that any battle fought to eliminate privilege and exploitation is in reality patriotic.

The Italian teacher finds himself regularly having to assign and correct compositions of a patriotic and fascist character. This is a task that even fascist professors find extremely embarrassing, because the students come to school with the finished paper in their pocket, or else they sprinkle it with ardent expressions of praise taken from the newspapers, confident that the professor will not be in a position to disapprove. Teachers are thus prevented from making any assessment of the value of the student.

Irritation and aversion toward topics on current affairs and the overblown rhetoric with which they are presented has therefore by now become widespread. Everyone feels the need to go back to concrete topics that allow an evaluation of the literary and historical thinking of the students and their ability to formulate and express their own ideas. The antifascist professor must be at the forefront of the fight against this rhetoric. This is a struggle that fascism will never be able to prohibit, and already some fascist newspapers sometimes find themselves championing this campaign.

Teaching History without Apologias

The antifascist Italian teacher can and must always mark as insufficient any composition compiled from set phrases taken from official apologias. Even while acquiescing in the assignment of compositions concerning politics, the professor must require substance, information and a knowledge of the factual data. He must cease to accept generalities and insist on a detailed knowledge of the historical, political and economic situation in question.

The highest marks will then go to the most accomplished and intelligent students, who will thus be pushed to see with their own eyes a truth that transcends journalistic formulas, a truth that often, especially to young people, speaks for itself.

It is the history curriculum that most regularly and insistently forces the teacher to come to grips with these arguments. The political subject par excellence, history contributes more than any other to forming young people's consciousness. It is essential to ensure, however, that it not become the most arid subject of all, and to think of it as unified with the history of culture, philosophy, economics and literature.

Antifascist professors mostly affirm their own principles in the glorification of certain historical figures, events, and periods. Their political leanings are applied to exalting the Athenian Tyrannicides, or Spartacus, Brutus, or Cato, or to taking the side of the Communards, the peasants' revolt, the Reformation, the Huguenots, Holland in the 1600s, America in the 1700s, and above all to praising the French Revolution and placing Mazzini at the center of the Risorgimento.

This is an attitude that is right, but not sufficient. This way, the students will know where the professor's sympathies lie and will make note of it. But they will not acquire actual criteria for historical judgment. History will remain for them an account of events and struggles in which you can take one side or the other according to your own tastes or your own current political interests. But it will still not represent the human reality from which we are directly descended and which has passed down to us a set of concrete situations and problems that we cannot escape.

If the professor's idea of history is limited to looking for a certain number of analogies with the present political situation, he will reduce his course to a series of allusions; he will basically be accepting, although inverting it, the fascist understanding of history as a continuous struggle between the principles of good and evil.

Now it is not necessary to be orthodox followers of historical materialism to have a more complete and organic vision of events than this and to recognize that economic and social factors are fundamental to political and cultural factors; to recognize, that is, that only a vision of these factors as dependent on one another can impart a vivid awareness of historical reality and link it with the present. This is indeed a conception that several official historians (Volpe, Rodolico, Gaggese) strongly influenced by Marxism followed in their best work, before they became fascists and before the genius De Vecchi arrived to set everyone straight and establish once and for all that each and every historical event was the exclusive work of the House of Savoy.[24]

Now the best way of giving a socialist or antifascist history course is to teach it in as complex and complete a way as possible, including all its social and economic connections; to see for example beneath the feudal economy and its derived social problems the substratum of the respective positions of the Empire and the Church and the culture that derived from them; to study the City-States, the Signoria, Humanism, the Renaissance, and the Reformation in relation to the new forces of the nascent bourgeoisie, the struggle of this bourgeoisie for political dominance, its position in relation to absolutism, its victory in the French Revolution, and the constitutional state as the political form that it bestowed on itself.

It is only when it has become a matter of course that historical facts and political ideologies are seen to be tightly bound to the social and economic world from which they arise, that students can be trained in a serious and concrete vision of the current political reality that will keep them from being duped by rhetoric and show instead that behind every gesture, every pose, and every legislative measure there is a set of needs that these things serve. Only then will the professor be able to talk of fascism without recourse to the hymns of praise that so revolt him and without the clumsy evasions that revolt the students, discussing it instead as a current historical phenomenon that can be analyzed in terms of its origins, its causes in the post-war crisis of the middle class, its agrarian and petty

---

[24]The kings of Italy.

bourgeois social makeup, its servitude in becoming the tool of Big Capital, and its reciprocal relations of support with the Monarchy and the Church. Only in this way can the origins of nationalism be sought in the ideologies of Bismark and of France in the early 20th century as distinct from the national unification movements of the 19th, showing the vitality and historical justification of the latter, and making it clear how today, now that national unification has arrived, the same words are being used and the same ideals exploited for purposes quite different from those that gave rise to them: purposes of imperialistic expansion that benefit no one but the big capitalists. This is the only way young people will come to understand how it is that in a Europe in which national problems have been almost completely resolved, the only point in stirring up national feelings that no longer have a real object to turn to is to distract attention from the real burning question of the age: the social problems within each country. This way they will also understand how, in the area of relations between one country and another, an ideology of all against all can be replaced with the ideology of cooperation of nation with nation, leaving to each the chance to resolve its own internal contradictions. This is the only way to set an ideal before the eyes of the young that includes the knowledge that they indeed belong to a national community, but that it has a function and meaning in the larger arena which is the human community. And in doing this, in my view, the schools should not (as they often do) show or imply a limitless admiration for democracies like France or England or the United States. In spite of holding on to their democratic forms of government, these were nevertheless the countries that introduced the concepts of imperialism and colonialism to the modern world and in the recent Abyssinian crisis it was clear that attempts to defend them found no resonance in the expectations of even the most unprejudiced young people. Undoubtedly, siding with one or the other of these countries is appropriate in certain political situations. But the task we can perform in the schools is more general. And it would be neither fair nor possible, talking to young people who see things with innocent, unprejudiced eyes, to deny that the present balance in Europe, built as it was by capitalist countries, is intended to preserve these countries' commercial and colonial privileges. This fact is there for all to see, and for a professor to challenge it would give his teaching a sectarian tone that would alienate the minds of his students.

Part II

1. OUR IMAGE[25]

Conceived as a letter to Silvia Colorni Schwartz, Eugenio's sister, "Our Image" is an incisive but charming essay that takes a personal event — the birth of Silvia, Ursula's and Eugenio's first daughter — as a special occasion for alerting us to the mistaken ideas we have about nature and, more generally, pointing out the "anthropomorphism" we are often not aware of. This essay was translated into English by Sarah and Albert Hirschman on the occasion of the birth of Alexander, the first son of Lisa (Sarah's and Albert's second daughter) and Peter Gourevitch on January 1st, 1978.

(1937)

Dear Silvia,

I write to give you good news about our little one. In the first month of her life, she has already grown by a pound. She sucks well, sleeps well, does not cry too much. She has begun to follow persons and things with her eyes and to have a special expression when she sees her mother. . . . During the first days I felt I was touching Providence with my own hands. Birth is an extraordinary phenomenon. The most complicated events happen with a regularity of a watch: frontal presentation, dilating pains, release of the water. Everything happens rapidly, logically, with precision. The baby is born. And everything is predisposed in such a manner that as soon as one mechanism of breathing ceases, another immediately takes over. The baby right away uses the new mechanism with utmost competence. Taken to the breast it sucks with a seriousness and commitment as though it had been years in training. During the first days the milk of the mother is not milk. It is a slightly laxative liquid, exactly the fluid the infant needs to rid the body of what is left over from the month of growth in the uterus. . . .

I said to myself, God Almighty must have thought a lot about us when he arranged all this. He combines everything just right. Ev-

[25]Now in Colorni, 2009, p. 270–74.

erything is so harmonious, coherent, economical. Everything has a purpose; nothing gets lost. There really must exist some "finalism" in nature that organizes matters along the simplest and best organized lines. No man-made machine can equal these natural mechanisms.

But I have had second thoughts when I have seen my wife tired out by the nursing and the nurses of the hospital busying themselves around my baby even though she was bursting with health. A little creature like that is capable of occupying a woman all day long.

I thought: "OK — I praised Providence for the things through which it has made my life easier. But why doesn't it occur to me to blame Providence for those things it has forgotten to arrange well for me?"

For what arcane end does nature obliges me to carry the baby in my arms for a whole year? To provide it with everything it needs, to keep it warm, to supply it with food, to change it seven times a day? If Providence has built such a beautiful machine to feed the child couldn't it also invent one to dry it? Nature is courteous and attentive insofar as the taking of the food is concerned. But how unhelpful it is with respect to the opposite function!

You may object that man himself with his civilization is responsible for these discomforts. Yet primitive people and animals experience similar difficulties. They too must take care of their children, feed them, protect them, clean them, teach them many things. They too receive some gifts from nature, but must work hard to supply themselves with those that they do not receive.

True enough, we find a certain order in some things. But we also note an enormous disorder in an immense number of others. All our labor consists in nothing but the attempt to remedy this disorder. In spite of that we call nature perfect and regular. As soon as, at some point, we see a bit of work already done for us, we fall to our knees and are ready to adore. . . . As far as I am concerned, I would be much more grateful to Providence if it had saved me not the initial laxative for my baby, but the continuous worry for his catching cold or getting too hot or becoming ill. . . .

Do not fear that I am embarking upon a dissertation on optimism and pessimism; that I want to decide whether the world is beautiful or ugly, or to side with Candide or Pangloss. I am asking a different question. Has nature arranged its laws to feed the needs of man or is it rather man who has taken advantage of a certain number of things in accordance with his needs and has arranged them to his convenience? And then . . . has said: "Here are the most perfect laws of nature as they have been arranged by Providence for my use." With these laws of his own making, man has built up his own concept of nature.

Man is unfazed when he meets with the irregular, the disorderly, the useless and noxious, and with all kind of phenomena whose purpose he is unable to decipher. Here too there is a law, he says, a most beautiful and perfect law. "It is so perfect that I am not yet strong enough to understand it. . . ." He has created words like 'contingency,' 'chance,' 'accident,' and others like 'mystery,' 'unknown,' 'inexplicable,' 'unexplored' . . . that precisely indicate that there is something there that he hopes one day to put to use for his own purposes. "It is a question of time," he says.

There is always a law, according to man. . . . I am sure that a scientist or a doctor would not be at all embarrassed by . . . these disappointments of a novice father. Everyone of the drawbacks about which I have complained is part of a marvelous order, once one knows how to look. It isn't the danger of my child being dropped and getting hurt the consequence of gravity, a universal law if there ever was one? And when the human body overheats or becomes too cold, does that also obey some quite precise rules? In so far as the whooping cough is concerned, the doctor assures me that science is hopeful of understanding the nature of this disease and of rendering it harmless. In short, man attempts to incorporate every disorder into some order, close or remote, present or future.

But what if there were a absolute, definitive, hopeless disorder? An area of experience that would now and always escape any kind of net, that would be impervious to every system and to every harmony? How would man behave in that eventuality? I cannot demonstrate to you that this kind of disorder exists in nature. What I can tell you is that if existed man would not notice it; he would pass next to it and would perhaps even touch it, but would not receive any impression from it.

Man does not have any organs suited for conceiving disorder.

And if he had, it would no longer be disorder; it would precisely enter into the system of his organs. Man has this specialty: to take notice only of what can be useful to him. . . . The irregular runs through his fingers — and that is the reason for which he says it does not exist.

Imagine that among many dots scattered about by chance, we isolate six that are symmetrically arranged and then we exclaim: "How marvelously nature has built the hexagon! How perfect is this figure! If one joins the vertexes with the center six equilateral triangles appear and they all are equal and the sum of all the angles is always equal to eight right angles! If one draws a circle around the hexagon, we can see that the side of the hexagon is equal to the radius of the circle! How clever we have been to uncover, in this chaos of dots, the monster of regularity! Surely, all the other dots will turn down to be similarly regular and all we need is to continue our efforts and we will find ever new harmonies!"

This is more the less the way we operate in the sciences. We choose among the immensity of the world some little tune that has about it a certain regularity (just as from a huge amount of noise we isolate sometimes a new sound that constitute a new melody). And we are incapable of hearing the rest. And it is that little tune that we call 'nature.' From birth, man is bound by a certain number of conditions that are simply there and are never questioned: two legs, two hands, two eyes, ten fingers, one heart. From that moment on he makes use of everything that corresponds to his mode of being and denies the existence of all that is unsuited to it. With what that turns out to be suited he builds his concepts and his values — beautiful and ugly, useful and noxious, good and evil. I assure you that if he had seventeen hands instead of two, symmetry, equilibrium, and proportion would be based on the number seventeen.

We see only what we look for, and we look only for what suits us. Little wonder then, that the world, as we are finding it, suits us. In this manner the myth arises that nature is beautiful and regular, or logical and mathematical. A myth which, as you know, is believed by both the materialistic scientist and the mystic.

Another example: you know that the animals after having given birth eat the placenta. We throw it away. . . . Because we think we know the function of this membrane, in our view it has had the purpose of enveloping the fetus. . . . But when the animal first saw this blood-stained thing he probably asked himself: "What is this thing good for? Let us try to eat it. . . ." Suppose now there were a scientist among the dogs or the horses: he would be convinced that the natural function of the placenta is to satiate the mother after giving birth. And he would exclaim: "How excellent a provider is nature; it provides our dogs and our horses with exactly the food they need and for which they crave."

Nature, believe me, is like a mirror that reflects the image of him who scrutinizes it. And man, the most intelligent of the animals, substitutes his own image for the mirror.

2. Letters to Ursula and Silvia

These excerpts of letters to his wife Ursula and to his sister Silvia from jail and internment (1938–1942) conceal a small treasury of sentiments, observations and fresh ideas that represent what might be called "Microfoundations" (as in the title chosen when a collection of quotes from Eugenio's personal letters was edited by Luca Meldolesi). They elucidate key points of Colorni's intellectual processes in literature, philosophy, psychology, physics, mathematics, geometry, biology etc. that lead him toward discoveries — in theory as well as practice.

Doubtfulness and Biology

Trieste, Sept. 21th 1938

My Dearest,

I'm reading *Faust*, one page per day, and to me the two prologues are better than Faust's famous monologue. What strikes me about Goethe is his — how can I put it? — his doubtfulness before he gives an opinion or makes a value judgement. Take the "Prologue in the Theatre." Are you really sure he agrees with the poet rather than the theatre director or the actor? OK, he agrees. But he seems to want to say: "I am capable of understanding the others' points of view as well. The way the others see things also 'exists.'" It's almost tragic when the actor tells him: you have your eye on posterity, but what about the living? Who's looking out for them? It's the same, basically, in the scene between God and Mephistofeles. In Goethe, as in Dante, Hell is more alive, more human than Heaven. (See De Sanctis's review.) But Faust's famous monologue, reading it again, was a bit disappointing: it's a bit pompous and started to get tiresome, that "living with all the senses" and "identifying with nature," etc. It's true that it was Goethe who invented it, but by now, for us, it's become commonplace. Schiller's byword is "judge," Goethe's is "understand." In this sense Goethe is more humble than Schiller. If all of this seems like nonsense, please tell me; and don't try to spare me because I'm in prison!

Then I went on reading *Il problema della Vita* [by Paolo En-riquez, Bologna: Zanichelli, 1937]. Either the book is badly con-structed (and partly, I think, it is) or we are in an area without guidelines, groping in the dark. There doesn't seem to be even the beginning of a uniform guideline in this biological research: the discoveries that are made seem basically random. In other words we're in the realm of physics before Galileo.

Still on the subject of the biology books you sent me, I see that scientists, in all their experiments, are still always stuck on this urge to create a homunculus, the man in the bottle. It's not exactly that, it's the synthetic formation of the living cell: but the principle, the ten-dency is the same: and what it is in fact is "remaking" with our own means what we find already made. Certainly up to now progress in science has happened in this way: artificially reconstructing a process found in nature (and machines are this and nothing else). But who can say that in the field of biology this isn't a mistaken and pointless course of action? Maybe we need something else altogether, some other "handle," some other way of approaching the problem?

Your Eugenio

"Genetic Knowledge" and Its Use

Varese, Nov. 14th 1938

My own Ursula,

You can imagine how I flung myself on the books you sent me, which came yesterday. They are everything to me and now that I have them I am better able to pass the time. Thanks also for your choices. You did very well; they just suit my tastes: a little physics, some classics, a little culture. When I was told that some books had arrived, I thought: I hope there's something by Goethe, and Peruc-ca's physics: and sure enough, there they were. It was also a great idea sending me some books on modern biology, a subject that I don't know at all and that I've wanted to read something about for a long time. In fact yesterday I immediately started *Il problema della Vita* by Federico Enriques, which seems very well done. The way the methods from the various sciences differ and yet always have starting points in common. What interests me more and more is to find reasons deriving from their physical and psychological makeup to explain why people have focused their attention on certain facts rather than others and considered some to be essential and others secondary. It's not so much "natural law" that interests me, but rather how people have come to formulate the regularity of nature precisely in the form of this law rather than some other. And I believe the meaning of this research is more than just philosophical; it is also and mainly scientific, because this "genetic" knowledge of natural law allows deeper penetration of its meaning and limitations, so that more appropriate use can be made of it. "Natural law" is not a reality, it is a tool. (Do you like this formulation?)

Since about a week ago I have been allowed a notebook and a pencil for a few hours each day, and I'm writing a physics-mathematics essay in which I think I've worked out some problems that I had been struggling with for some time. Yesterday evening I also started reading *Don Quixote* and I'll write more to you about it later.

Now, my dearest, I would like to offer you a little sermon; because it seems to me that you are letting yourself fall into a state of apathy and drowsiness that I don't like at all. You know that for the two of us boredom is not an option. And I think you need to busy yourself with something and lead a more active life. Why not think about your thesis? Or if not that, read, or write, or do sports, or anything really: but keep busy. You know that sometimes you have to tie yourself perhaps a bit artificially to a job or study something that doesn't satisfy you a hundred percent. (Like I did for years with my work on Leibniz). But if you don't do this, the moment for something that really does capture your interest will never arrive. You seem always to be waiting for inspiration, for the occupation that will give you unreserved joy. But this will never arrive if you don't prepare for it yourself with a training program that tests you a bit.

As you can see, the books you sent have turned me back into the old grouch.

Your Eugenio

Theoretical Work as a Tool for Understanding

Varese, Nov. 26th 1938

My dearest, don't trouble yourself over the sermon I gave you last week; it was because I had got the idea that you were a bit ap-

athetic and unhappy and bored; and I thought a little encourage-
ment from me might help you fight off your depression. But you
know I just want you to be contented and happy — and not only
for the usual obvious reasons but because I know that when you are
happy you know how to experience your happiness so deeply and
intensely that whatever you do, even if it's the most mundane thing,
you know how to find beauty and spiritual richness in it. Remember, in any case, if you ever feel a little tired and down and you feel
like you are living a life that isn't very interesting, remember that
the experiences of the most interesting people who ever lived are
concentrated in books, and if you look hard you can always find a
book that at that moment fits your mood.

My health is fine. I'm studying physics from Perucca's book;
in the evening I read the biology books, and then to bed with *Don
Quixote*. By now I've almost finished the biology books. But I hav-
en't experienced that sense of new doors opening that you get reading the books on the new physics. The research is still chaotic and
doesn't seem to have found its proper way yet. And I get the feeling that a large part of the theoretical work in this field (vitalism,
mechanism, evolution, natural selection, etc.) has a purpose that
you might call gratuitous — that is, they don't lead to advances in
research, or to getting new results; their purpose is mainly to satisfy
the need people have for complete theories that solve problems in
bulk, a need that to me is not very attractive. Take, for example,
the famous problem of "vital energy." I wouldn't be particularly opposed to the use of this concept (in the way it is useful to talk about
"thermal energy" or chemical or electrical energy). But in order to
decide whether to use it or not you have to ask: "Will this concept
help us understand things better, discover new facts or interpret old
ones in a simpler and more systematic way, formulate useful laws
that open the way to new predictions and applications?" If so, then
by all means let's welcome the concept of vital energy. It is its success, what it can achieve, that determines whether a concept ought
to be accepted. Instead, I have the idea that generally arguments for
or against a concept are based on inclinations or feelings that have
nothing to do with searching for truth.

I am reconciling myself somewhat with my old and abandoned

field of philosophy. For this reason I'm keeping back the Simmel book as the "dulcis in fondo," saving the best for last. What I mean is, I still detest philosophy as a way of consoling oneself in the face of evil, making up for losses, satisfying curiosity, replacing tidbits that are no longer available. This is why I detest any philosophical system that seeks to "close the circle" and explain the universe to you. But philosophy as a tool, as a ray of light that clarifies misunderstandings and removes prejudices still seems indispensable. And in the end comes down simply to exercising intelligence and honesty.

Your Eugenio

Understanding vs. Explaining

Varese, Nov. 28th 1938

My dearest,

I've started the Simmel book and so far I'm a bit disappointed. Always the same stories of the spirit as a continuous surpassing of oneself, a setting and overcoming of limits, etc. Variations on a theme that has by now been worked to death. It's strange how hard it is to find an observation, even a tiny one, that's fresh and honest, and that opens up a new point of view to you! I think the problem is in the approach: that philosophers are basically not very interested in "understanding," but are overly concerned with "explaining." And often these two things are contradictory. Explaining in fact means finding such and such a theory or system or organization of reality in which everything has its place and in which there is a place for everything. Understanding means facing things, you might say, in a state of passivity, ready to grasp them in the way that presents itself as most appropriate. This is why I like Goethe. "Systems" for him were not really serious things. In fact he must have changed them many times in his life. A "system" for him was nothing but an amusing game. The important thing, the serious thing was "understanding," in any way and with whatever method. I would like to read Nietzsche.

As you see, I am always circling around the same ideas. But I don't believe they are useless to me or to my scientific research.

Keep sending me your observations on people in the family, which amuse me no end. You show me a complete picture of attitudes that I had always only been half aware of, because these are people I have known from birth, and I have no detachment from. But these scenes you set out are so true!

Getting back to the discussions on philosophy in our last letters, I can tell you that probably the main thing that took me away from systematic and professional philosophy was having married you. Basically, I was always extremely embarrassed in front of you over my interminable Leibniz. In order to do this sort of work, you have to live a little bit separate from the world in a clique of people who, following university convention, give great importance to these things so as to create the illusion for themselves that they are profound etc. There are people who live their whole lives behind fences of this kind: literati, professors, nearly all of them. But then you happen to find yourself with a person from the real world, and you see in their eyes the question: "Well, but what good is it?" And you realize that the answer that you cooked up long ago for this question, which made such a good impression at home, or at school, or in the university environment, doesn't take hold with the people "in the world" whose esteem you crave — it just sounds false. This is basically what happened with you. I realized that the whole circle of issues that my Leibniz revolved around was valid in that artificial and professional environment, but sounded empty in the world outside. By this I don't mean to deny the value of scientific professionalism. But some of it is just tail-chasing.

The example you give is really good, about "not being able to live with two gauches" [two lefts]. In these times I too always think about mystical conceptions and philosophical systems, as if a child who wants the moon were given a paper-mâché moon by his over-indulgent parents, and he goes around boasting and saying: "I have the moon." And to anyone who notes that there are good reasons to believe that this is not in fact the moon, he replies: "But I can't live without the moon, so this is the moon." This "not being able to live without" is exactly the point where the arbitrariness of these conceptions shows up.

Your Eugenio

Disappointment with Simmel

Varese, Dec. 8th 1938

[to Ursula]

Simmel's book, which I am reading slowly, gives me contrasting impressions. Sometimes he says beautiful, incisive things and then just leaves them there, content with having described them, without using them or applying them. He has some interesting observations, for example, concerning the processes by which the mind attributes to certain types of activity their own autonomy as ends in themselves (art, morals, etc.). But then? Think how much psychology could be done based on this — for example, dissecting the process of needs, tendencies and fears that such an attitude derives from! And Simmel instead (like all the philosophers) gives us nothing — he is content to have described this with a formula, to have framed it in a system, in a law — this satisfies him completely. I will never get tired of repeating it: a law has a purpose only if it is put to use. If all it does is satisfy us it is useless.

Your Eugenio

The More Man Dominated Nature, the Less He Felt Like the Master

Varese, Dec. 12th 1938

My dearest Ursula,

Everything comes with philosophy. The fact is, there's nothing for me to do here except study and think about philosophical ideas. And it's really true, and I told you this last time as well, that I stole these ideas from you. And it's also true that to teach something, words are no use; what you need is love. The fact is, you have never preached against philosophy to me; on the contrary, you have always tried very hard to understand my thoughts and my studies. But your efforts to accept their usefulness, and mine to demonstrate it to you, have led me to understand — or, I should say, to feel — that you are right. It's like this: to convince someone that they are wrong you have to try, with great effort and with great love, to agree with them (that is, to understand them). It is only from this mutual effort to understand one another that love is nurtured and the truth comes out. And so I sometimes feel remorse at having too feebly and too rarely made this effort to "agree with you"; and sometimes when I did so it was with too cold a sense of justice.

Reading your letter last night I had the idea that I should out-line for you the general drift of my philosophy. So here goes (noth-ing new or ground-breaking, I hasten to say): Humans have made true progress whenever they notice that they are not the center of the universe. The case of Copernicus is the most typical and striking, but throughout the history of civilization there are these "leaps outside ourselves," this awareness that the laws that we had attributed to reality were, in essence, nothing other than an imag-ined reality created in our image and likeness as a good servant of our needs. Every time a step like this has been taken mankind has gained understanding from it and engaged better with reality, and powerful tools with which to control nature have fallen into our hands. The more man has dominated nature, the less he has felt like its master, its central figure. And here again you might say it took much more "love" and less "pride" to achieve this un-derstanding. You could say that the entire evolution of thought, from primitive people who attributed rain and sunshine to the will of the gods — that is, to men who were bigger and stronger than themselves — down to Plato, who attributed reality and ob-jective truth to our minds, and to Newton, who held that space and time were real entities, made progress every time the world of "essence" was replaced by that of "relations." But to do this requires an immense effort of honesty and, you might say, of asceticism. It requires the courage to look at ourselves as if we were outside our-selves, to become our own objects of observation (and this is the connection with the dialectic), to give up our habits of thinking. In this sense, morals and science are the same thing. And every scientific discovery, I would say even every technical achievement, is like a slap in the face that says: things are not the way my model would like them to be organized. It is precisely for this reason that every discovery is necessarily incomplete, and that it is pointless to construct vast systems in which everything is well organized. Every discovery is like growing from a child into an adult and say-ing: "How foolish I was! I thought the moon was a toy made just to entertain me." Essentially, it's an exercise in humility. You might reply: okay, but this is a method like any other. But no: I support this method because it is the only one that yields results. Whoever has applied this method has been enriched with knowledge and tools, and entire regions of the natural world have opened up. They have a nice little saying, the philosophers: our research is disinterested; we don't care about concrete results. But concrete results are the only evidence we have that we are on a track that will be productive for everybody. Otherwise this so-called disinterest on the part of philosophers just turns out to be an interest in satisfying their curiosity or allaying their fears. The point that modern physics has latched onto, with the enormous results it has achieved, is precisely this: Space, time and motion are not "Platonic ideas," nor are they realities in themselves — they are relations. And in this regard there are two things that strike me: 1. How exhausting it has been to remove these preconceptions from people — a sign that they were deeply rooted not only intellectually but, I would say, almost organically. 2. The incredible breadth of the landscape that has opened up to human eyes with the removal of these concepts.

I will stop here, my darling. They are old ideas, I know, but it does me good to tell you them.

Your Eugenio

Every Discovery Is a Reversal of a Point of View
                                        Varese, Dec. 13th 1938

Dear sister,

My health is good and, relatively speaking, so is my mood. I realize that the only way to suffer less from the solitude and separation is to keep my mind occupied; and for me, since I'm in the habit of spending long hours at my desk, this comes more easily, so that sometimes, when I'm working out my ideas and thoughts, I almost forget the situation I'm in, and I need to remember to look around. But this also makes me afraid that I've become a terrible bore, unable to write about anything other than criticism, science and philosophy. Well, grant me this at least; that way when we're together again I can go back to being the clown. So if you happen to have problems, ideas, inquiries, questions, doubts, uncertainties, requests, curiosities and the like, feel free to write to me, because here you will find the true, infallible oracle. "If doubts torment and assail you, or even if they don't, ask me, readers, and I will answer." The words, if I'm not mistaken, of Bertoldo. And in fact it is perfectly fitting — an oracle from the depths of a prison. So write to me if you want to have a chat, and I hope you will perhaps find me more understanding and more willing to understand than I have been in the past. Speaking of newspaper comics, to me they are most definitely a great source of wisdom. For a number of months, years even, I have been mulling over a cartoon that I would like to make almost the motto of my philosophy. There are two sunflowers and one says to the other, "The latest studies have shown that it isn't the sun that always moves to where we're looking, but it's us who always turn to face the sun." Well, we laugh at the sunflowers, but if you think about it, up until four hundred years ago people acted exactly the same way, believing that the sun revolved around the earth! And they still do the same thing today in an infinite number of cases! The way I see it, every discovery, every step forward, is a reversal of point of view just like the sunflowers.'

Please don't sigh if I've already told you this story. You have to forgive me everything now, thinking, poor guy, in these conditions. . . . But don't get the idea that all I do is mull over these theories. On the contrary, this is only a side line. My main focus is on trying to apply them scientifically. Take this, for example: modern physics has demolished the concepts of absolute space and time, absolute motion, etc. But it has kept the concept of a "universal constant." Well I think this concept can be demolished just like absolute motion, and this demolition can lead to new and productive scientific developments.

Your Eugenio

Nietzsche's Way of Expressing Himself

Ventotene, April 8th 1939

My Dearest Pini,

I sleep a lot. I work quite a bit, but more in the philosophical-literary sense than the scientific-mathematical; which I'm sorry about, because I don't want to lose my edge. I read Nietzsche [*Beyond Good and Evil* 1886], and I find all the ideas that I've thought of, but expressed in a different way and irreparably sterile. Why?

I think it's because he expressed them in anger, resentfully, without thinking about applying his ideas in any concrete and useful way, and all besotted with the courage he showed in daring to say these things. On every page you find at least ten times the words "wagen" [risk], "Tapferkeit" [courage], etc. So that his philosophy, entirely correct, remained sterile, a perfect example of intelligence and heartlessness, and nothing more.

Eugenio

A Psychology for the Healthy

Ventotene, May 11th 1939

My Dearest,

As for what you say about psychology and the unconscious, you seem to be taking back everything you've taught me. Hadn't we reached the point (with difficulty, in my case) of saying that the literal sense of a word doesn't mean anything? That every word is like a flower in your buttonhole? That is, that its value comes from a certain indefinable "intentionality"? Now it is surely true that very often even though you know rationally, as a fact, the origin of a tic, this doesn't mean you are cured of it. Now I maintain that knowing in this way is not true knowing: it's knowing a "fact," not reliving the experience in your memory, being ashamed of it down to the most intimate fiber of your being, etc. Therefore, as a rule, when the doctor gives you the explanation for your tic and you too recognize that it's correct and accept it, you still don't feel cured. The new psychology gives you not only a new definition of knowing (which in itself amounts to nothing), but also reveals a new way of knowing, until now hidden: and that is "remembering being ashamed." And you realize that this new type of knowing (and this alone) gets rid of nervous tics. All philosophy had always suspected that lying beneath rational and empirical knowledge there was another type of knowledge that was deeper, more intimate and close-fitting, an "Erleben" [experience]. Now we have a method of reaching this type of knowledge, and (most importantly) we have a criterion for recognizing whether this type of knowledge has actually been achieved: and that is, if it led to the disappearance of tics, complexes, needs, etc., then it was in fact that new type of knowledge; otherwise, it wasn't; otherwise it was simply the usual rational and empirical knowledge of "factual data."

I would say that the new psychology is much more useful to the healthy than to the sick. In sick people arriving at this "remembering being ashamed" is extremely difficult, always bound to the person of the doctor who often, without meaning to, can influence the patient; everything can often (as you say) come down to a phenomenon of autosuggestion, and in the best case can do no more than eliminate a couple of tics. Healthy people, on the other hand (or rather, relatively healthy people, since there is no such thing as a completely healthy person) are free of the doctor's influence because they have no doctor, and the role of the doctor is played (so to speak) by the infinite shocks and encounters that life presents; and any doctor will be dominated by a healthy person rather than vice versa. And what will be achieved is not only the elimination of a couple of tics, but this new type of experience and knowledge, which can then be put to use in various ways. In Nietzsche all this is clearly indicated; indeed it may be said that all this is no more than a realization of Nietzsche's program.

Your Eugenio

Against the Category of 'Reality'

Ventotene, May 17th 1939

My Dearest Ursula,

My health is good, and I get lots of sun in the afternoon stretched out on the deck chair. I've now got back a bit to my physics studies and slowed down on the philosophy: alternating like this I never get bored. I notice more and more that all my research in physics is dominated by a concept, essentially philosophical, which is: the destruction of the category of "reality." Once you eliminate this concept, wherever it hides, in the formulations of the natural sciences, you reach transformations and results that to me seem interesting. Now a careful investigation of this need or demand for "reality," which is after all one of the essential categories in human thought, reveals that it is due to a set of complexes and reactions to adversity, but mainly to the complex that I would call "fear of being deceived." These complexes are the source of the human spirit of inquiry, research and curiosity — in a word, science. When these complexes become pathological, and need to be satisfied at all costs, they give rise to theosophies. Now in my case these complexes have always been very weak (while in Silvia they are very strong); and therefore when I read Kant's affirmation that space and time and causality etc. are not realities in themselves but rather expressions of our thinking, it satisfied me completely and met with no resistance. This I would say is the only thing I've learned from philosophy; and it is the nucleus around which my thinking has continued to revolve.

Your Eugenio

Systems and Discoveries

Ventotene, May 20th 1939

Dearest,

Today I'm really down and in bad mood and I'm fed up with this constant writing to each other; I just want to be with you and hold your hand and not say anything, with our little ones playing around us. Ok, we'll dispense with the melancholy. It's raining here today. Now I'll reply to your ideas: I agree with you completely that everything is psychology and that the cardinal error is taking words as "absolute." For example, it is common to talk about "the will" as if it were something unitary and indivisible, and easy to understand. And the fact is, behind the word "will" a multitude of processes are gathered, each different from the others, each very complicated and divisible into various parts. And philosophy speaks of "the will" as if it were a simple and intuitive thing, indivisible like an atom, comprising the "raw material" that the spirit is made of! As for your suspicions about the cataract operations, I can say that I don't believe in systems either, but I do believe, wholeheartedly, in "discoveries." The discovery of electricity opened up an enormous field of applications, it made us vastly richer; and this happened all at once, in the course of a few decades. Now I consider the new psychology to be about on a par with the discovery of electricity. It has put into our hands a set of mechanisms that allow us to construct and demolish many things. First application: a cure for several nervous disorders. But there are also other possible applications. Curing nervous disorders is the control experience, you might say, that demonstrates that in general the method works. The idea now is to find the fields in which this method is applicable and can yield good results. And we must resist the temptation to turn this method into a system, a philosophy; that is, it has to be used in areas where it works and only there.

Your Eugenio

The Moralist and the Scientist

Ventotene, May 22th 1939

My Dearest,

I'll tell you something I've been thinking recently: a person can be attracted to philosophy for two intimate reasons: the fear of being unclean (or of being exposed). Or the fear of being deceived. The first produces the moralist, and the second the theorist and the scientist (I would be the first type). Let me explain: the first type is the person who needs to be clean at all costs, who is constantly afraid of a rigid and implacable eye that judges and condemns all his actions (conscience), who needs a stability that can guarantee that he is upright, honest and clean.

These needs give rise to the categorical imperative, the action as an end in itself, etc. This person takes up philosophy as a guide, a safe refuge against his own weakness. — In the other case, there is a certain craving to know "how things really are," a curiosity about what is "real," a need to search for the "real" beneath the "appearances." This is the case for people who have been afraid of being deceived ever since they were children, who looked down on fairy tales and wanted "true" stories; who then went on to become fanatical about taking toys apart to discover how they worked, the investigators, researchers, experimenters. For them it is not morals but knowledge that is an end in itself.

When these needs are so overpowering that they fill someone's entire soul, this is when they're drawn to philosophy or pure science as a vocation. But as you've seen, this vocation isn't really anything but a need for defense, a struggle to free oneself from fear. People's vocations therefore push them precisely in the direction where they are most constrained by their complexes, where they are less agile and relaxed. And where they have fewer complexes, where they are agile and relaxed, they feel no impulse to act, precisely because they feel no need to defend themselves, to seek safety. There they feel no "vocation."

Something like this is what has happened to your husband, who is tightly bound to the "staying clean" side, but quite relaxed on the "not being deceived" side. If it is now possible for someone to escape from their first vocation, which pulled them in the direction of psychological "slavery," this will liberate a great deal of energy that can be used on the side where they are more free and relaxed. So what's happening to me is that, freed of the impulses that were pushing me toward philosophy, and turning toward the field of science, I constantly run into researchers and scientists all occupied with fixations that I don't understand, all concerned about "reality," which doesn't matter to me in the slightest. And it often seems to me that their problems are nonexistent, all just made up to satisfy this famous obsession with reality.

And I wonder: if someone were to follow this path backwards, starting with this reality fixation, and were to break free of it and turn toward the field which for them had from the start been free of fixations, the field of morality and the categorical imperative, what would they find? What would they build?

Your Eugenio

An Experimental Morality

Ventotene, May 24th 1939

My Dearest Pini,

I can't tell you the joy your letter of the 20th gave me, not only because of what you wrote, but because it seems to me from the way you write that you are better and stronger, and it lifted the worries I had from your previous letters about your health. Since yesterday evening I've been constantly thinking over the ideas you wrote about and last night I put together a number of answers which I'm not sure I have time to write down in the hour I have left before the post goes out.

So let me say that this idea of a rich, prodigal natural world that needs to be wasteful, that sets in motion immense forces to

achieve meager results etc., is another of the ideas that our friend
Nietzsche stole from you. And as an idea it is worth about as much
as the (diametrically opposed) idea of nature as thrifty and always
directed toward a goal, a realm where everything has a purpose,
nothing is wasted, everything has its place etc. The one idea is
worth exactly as much as the other; that is, nothing. Or, let's say,
they may be partly true, both of them; but they're of no utility
whatsoever. In fact, everything known as "work" or "intelligence"
in humans is directed toward defending us against these two laws
— that is, toward creating order where nature has created none, or
taking the disorganized and chaotic processes nature has roughed
out and making them more economical and profitable, more "us-
able." We are "savers" where nature has been a "spendthrift." It is
true that nature follows tortuous pathways to arrive at an outcome,
but it isn't true that when humans find a "direct route" they are
constrained to make use of it only by means of these convoluted
paths. Let science guide us: mechanics and electricity are "direct
routes," and it does seem that for two thousand years humanity
endlessly went in circles and achieved very little (in this field), but
that once we embarked on the direct route we had the possibility of
breaking through immediately, at dizzying speed. Now if it is true
that the direction I'm headed in today represents a "direct route,"
the thing to do is not to make the moment of illumination drag out
until eternity (in other words, construct a system), but rather to
make the most of the direct route. There is a big difference between
"interpreting a discovery philosophically" and "putting a discovery to use," and the second of these is what I would like to do. And
I do realize that this leaves an impression of pettiness and lack of
generosity, but I think that essentially all of science might come
down to "economizing" (that is, moving more quickly, looking
further ahead, becoming stronger, exploiting the riches of nature).
This is why I believe it is not wrong benefit from a creative act. In
a certain sense, what I would like to do is something like propaganda for a mental attitude. Every philosophical system is a way of
advocating for an idea, for the brilliant intuition at its centre. It's
saying: Look, you'll be fine if you adopt this way of seeing things,
you'll resolve all your problems, you'll know how you should be-

have, you will truly know yourself and others, you will be able to make judgments about art, morals, etc. In short, you will find the answers to many of the doubts, mysteries and fears that torment you. For myself, I couldn't care less about doubts and fears. My way of advocating is different. I say: Look, if you adopt this way of seeing things you will be able to split the atom, build machines and predict astronomical phenomena. The publicity I'm doing is technical. The philosopher promises you your peace of mind (a house of cards), the scientist promises you riches and dominion over nature (an open room in the real house). What I like and what truly impresses me is that I think I have clarified for myself the process by which a certain psychological and moral attitude can lead to a scientific discovery; in such a way that the discovery almost constitutes the experimental confirmation of the utility of the original attitude. And it's precisely this process that I would like to describe: a sort of "experimental morality." Something like in children's fairy tales: "If you leave your arrogance behind and forget your pride, then the treasure house will open and the fairy will appear before you in all her beauty."

I see the time is almost up. Goodbye sweetheart, you don't need to write to me. Just stay well and don't tire yourself too much. And don't forget there's someone here who thinks of you and our little ones always.

Your Eugenio

Freeing Oneself from the Slavery of Words
Ventotene, May 25th 1939

My Dear,

I'm constantly thinking about the things you wrote to me. The concept of philosophy as a sort of hidden biography of the author is precisely what Nietzsche thought. And that phrase of Baudelaire's that you sent is exactly the opposite of what I think. I think that everything that's wrong with metaphysics (which shows up not only in philosophy, but also everywhere in daily life) comes precisely from taking words as something sacred, forgetting that they are tools and are always approximations. Kant (the only philosopher I truly love) was brave enough to free himself from the myth of "reality," but not from the myth of "words." He had the courage to say that space, time, substance and causality do not represent anything real, but he did not have the courage to say that they are just tools, valuable only so long as they are useful. He said: we are bound to them, they constitute the necessary essence of our being, which is to say: they are not Reality (with a capital R), but they are "Words" (capital W). Freeing oneself from philosophy (or at least from what has been called philosophy up to now) means freeing oneself from the capital letters, that is from the slavery of words. And to do this, to speak always in small letters, requires agility, ease, grace, modesty, good taste, simplicity, and honesty beyond compare.

Your Eugenio

Four Ways of Philosophizing

Ventotene, June 1st 1939

My Urselchen,

If you knew what pleasure and consolation I get from what you write, that the only philosopher you understand is Kant. . . . And I also feel shock and anger against Fichte and Schelling and Hegel, who really did ruin the achievement of his thinking, which they cut down to nothing. What is infuriating is the thought that basically these are people who are sick with the philosophical disease, this need to close the circles and this fear of being caught in the open, etc. And instead of recognizing that they are ill and trying to get better, or creating little personal shelters where they can live peacefully, suffer less and not be so afraid, they puff their little shelters up, wave them to the four winds and use them to make careers and become celebrities. What you write about the 30 dice and about the noumenon as a tender spot that they stupidly rage against is perfect. The noumenon is the final tribute Kant pays to the philosophical need to close circles. And they jump all over it: "no, that's not how you close the circle, you do it in a different way." I don't know if I ever told you this fable that comes to mind. A father leaves his children in the house, saying "Here you'll find everything you need, but you'll be in real trouble if you try to go outside. You'll be naked and helpless in the street, with nobody to come to your aid." The children split up. There's one who uses the house, but who every so often looks wistfully out the window overlooking the forbidden street (positivist scientists like Spencer, Comte, Poincaré, and regret for the "unknowable"). Another (the mystic) breaks the lock and runs out into the street where, without seeing or understanding anything, he claims to have found the solution to all the problems that existed in the house, presenting the street as a bigger and more beautiful house. Another (the modern scientist) tries to fit wheels onto the house and modify it so that it is possible to move along the streets without ever leaving the house. And what do you think the last one does? He bars the doors, closes the shutters, and declares: the street doesn't exist: the whole world begins and ends inside the house. And this last one — the stupidest of all, the one with the least imagination, the sickest — this is the idealist philosopher, like Hegel and Fichte. Leibniz and Descartes, as a type, are a bit different. They really did have something to say both in the field of science (one invented infinitesimal calculus, the other analytical geometry) and in scientific methodology. Only they preferred, for reasons of convenience, to express these things in the language then in use, a theological-systematic language. Therefore, to understand them it is necessary to "translate" from that systematic language to ours. Once this is done, the theses and demonstrations that appear to be senseless games take on an important meaning, one that is in no way systematic. The introduction to my book is a simple biography and won't help you understand Leibniz; what you need is the first part (my anthological exposition) of the book, but it's a little long. Maybe in one of my next letters, if you like, I can write you a brief summary of his philosophy. Something short and sweet perhaps, for the moment I'm not sure. At this point I believe in it so little that I just can't seem to focus my mind on it. But send me a list of subjects you'd like me to ramble on about, and I will do so at once.

For Leibniz and Descartes, perhaps what you need, more than my book, is that communication on the "Eternal Ideas in Descartes and Leibniz"[26] that, if I'm not mistaken, you typed a copy of for me. It's an attempt at that "translation" that I was telling you about. But

---

[26]Colorni, 2009, p. 83–92.

the one who really took Descartes at his word and tried to pursue the ultimate consequences of his thought and close the circle, with a level of diligence and commitment that I don't know whether to call ingenuous, ridiculous, or monstrous, is Spinoza. And with this I proclaim: a) that it's almost nine, the hour when they now sound the retreat; b) that the chocolates, alas, are gone; c) that I'm in a good mood thanks to your letter.

Eugenio

3. Commodo to Ritroso

In Ventotene Colorni discussed many topics with Altiero Spinelli, Ernesto Rossi (a well-known economist), Ursula Hirschmann and others. Often at night some of them carried on those discussions as written dialogues (Now collected as E. Colorni and A. Spinelli, Dialoghi di Ventotene). One of them, titled "On Psychologism in Economics"[27] written by Colorni as a dialogue between Commodo-Colorni and Ritroso-Rossi, was long considered inachevé. But recent findings by Geri Cerchiai provide a surprise: the very valuable one, from which we propose an excerpt.

On Economics and Method

Palinode[28]

Right from the start I got myself into a serious rage and I answered you in an insolent letter. But then, re-reading everything in a calmer frame of mind, I saw that in the end you were perfectly right. But since your accusations do affect me only in a certain particular way, I want to explain the following to you purely as a personal clarification:

It is right to expect someone who approaches a science he does not know to do so "with a humble mind"[29] — ready to learn, that is, rather than to criticize. It requires, and quite rightly, a long and silent apprenticeship, and it is only at the end of this that he can grant himself a place in the conversation.

All this is right (and I say it without the slightest irony). But the result is that a person usually does only one of these apprenticeships and then remains stuck with it for the rest of his life. You specialize in a subject and never leave it, except for amateur excur-

---

[27]Colorni, 2019, p. 188–89.
[28]Retraction of what was expressed previously
[29]In the original: "con le ginocchia della mente," free quotation from "Vergine bella che di sol vestita" (Petrarca, 2012, p. CCCLXVI) [note by Geri Cerchiai].

sions taken out of curiosity.

This is not allowed to me at the moment, since my most specific interests are directed toward the methodology of the sciences. And since it would appeal me to apply a top-down solution to the problem, devising a couple of philosophical criteria and treating them as keys that would open all doors, I am forced to approach each science not seeking to learn about it generically, but committed rather to observing its internal mechanisms with a critical eye and drawing conclusions that are not philosophical in general terms, but which can help the science itself to move forward. If I want to do this, it's clear that I can't expect to escape the most demanding apprenticeship in each of the sciences I approach. And I wouldn't dream of escaping. But I can try to make the experience more enjoyable. The method I have unconsciously found is this:

Rather than passively cozying up to ponderous treatises, all ready to settle in and learn the material just the way it is presented, I start out with my lance at the ready, full of wrongheaded, confused ideas, breaking down doors at every step, inventing shields, eager for clashes and battles. I emerge from every one of these engagements bruised and battered (as in this case) but with clearer ideas. Every knock-out takes me a step closer to understanding the science. I don't avoid studying, of course, and I do read the treatises: but it is more enjoyable to me to read them as if they were impassioned fighters rather than loving pedagogues. With the understanding, of course, that there will be no foot-stamping; one must be ready to recognize defeat.

4. The Project for a Journal of Scientific Methodology[30]

In the spring of 1942, Eugenio wrote the following "Project" and brief-
ly explained the meaning of it in a letter to Ursula (see "Annex" be-
low). He discussed it at length with Ludovico Geymonat and sent him
the framework and some outlines. In this breathtaking project, the-
ories and discoveries (in physics and math, biology and psychology,
economics and statistics etc.) are observed so that their influence on
philosophical concepts and problems may be studied; and vice versa,
the evolution of the latter is utilized to speed up developments in the
former. This is part of Colorni's campaign against anthropomorphism,
which he considered the n. 1 enemy of the development of science.

General Character

The journal need not be of an informative nature since two
excellent examples of this already exist: *Scientia* and *Il Saggiatore*.[31]
Its character should be critical and philosophical. Whether there is
theoretical justification for the expression "scientific philosophy"
as opposed to "philosophy of science," and whether or not this represents an independent attitude of the mind is of little concern to
us. For us it is sufficient that the field of study corresponding to
this name be quite clearly delimited. Generally speaking, it ought
to include all questions in principle related to sciences that make
use of experimental methods and scientific tools. It follows that in
addition to physics and mathematics, which should provide most
of the topics covered, the biological and psychological sciences
should also be represented, along with economics and statistics

---

[30]The text, datable to 1942, was published in *Scritti,* Bobbio, ed., 1975, pp. 239–42 and,
later, in E. Curiel and E. Colorni, *Il sogno di una nuova Italia,* edited by M. Quaranta,
presented by F. Zanonato, Edizioni Sapere, Padova 2005. The complete reference for the
quote from Alberto V. Geremicca cited by Colorni is as follows: *Spiritualità nella natura.*
Istinto, ereditarietà, intelligenze, sviluppo ed evoluzione, Laterza, Bari 1939 [note by G.
Cerchiai, 2009: 176].
[31]*The Rivista di scienza* founded in 1907 by Federico Enriques and a small group of scientists, became *Scientia* in 1909. *Il Saggiatore. Rivista mensile di attualità scientifica* was
published for only two years, from 1940 to 1942, by Einaudi (note by G. Cerchiai 176).

insofar as they seek to build for themselves a logical tool based on axiomatic fundamentals.

There are two points of view from which the topics may be approached:

(1) Studying the extent to which the development of scientific theories and discoveries influences philosophical concepts and problems (for example: space, time, causality, equality, object, the individual, etc., for the physical sciences; life, the will, the self, guilt, for the psychological and biological sciences).

(2) Showing how a thorough analysis of the basic principles of the various sciences, in which all the achievements of philosophical thought are brought into play, can be useful to the sciences themselves and contribute to their progress.[32]

Part I. Articles and Essays

The cooperation of leading Italian and foreign scientists could be sought, as long as they contributed articles of a critical nature and not expositions of scientific discoveries and theories. Much space should instead be given to presenting the leading interpretive and methodological tendencies.

The articles could be separated into the following groups; for each I will give some topics, as examples.

(a) Basic articles:

On the concept of experience.

---

[32]One of the features of Colornian epistemology is to study scientific methodology starting from the problem of science itself. Cf. what Guido Morpurgo Tagliabue wrote to Norberto Bobbio: "All his [Colorni's] attention was focused on problems of physical-mathematical science, a current topic in those years [. . .]. This helps explain a particular fact: that this student of philosophy chose to approach the problem of science not through epistemology, as would have seemed obvious, but through an immediate, albeit incipient, contact with the actual work of science" (letter of G. Morpurgo Tagliabue to N. Bobbio, Milan, 31 March 1974, cited in S. Gerbi, *Tempi di malafede. Una storia italiana tra fascismo e dopoguerra. Guido Piovene ed Eugenio Colorni*, Einaudi, Torino 1999, p. 97; Bobbio resumed his evaluation of Morpurgo Tagliabue in his Introduction to Colorni's writings, p. xxv). If this proposition implies, as Colorni of the anti-philosophical polemic has it, a neglect of the more strictly philosophical problems, it is a question that is addressed by the author in various places in his writings, but which finds a partial answer in his awareness, shown in these pages, that he is in any case doing research of a "critical-philosophical" nature [note by G. Cerchiai, 2009: 177].

Universal constants and units of measurement.

The finalist illusion in physics.

The finalist illusion in biology.

The realist illusion in physics.

Geometry and experience.

On the axiomatics of the principles of mechanics.

On the axiomatics of the theory of relativity.

On the axiomatics of quantum mechanics.

Precision physics and field physics.

On the concept of instinct.

On the present state of the argument between mechanical determinism and vitalism.

Is it possible to build an economy independent of psychological assumptions?

(b) Profile of leading contemporary thinkers, both scientists who have been guided in their work by methodological considerations and philosophical interpreters of scientific doctrine:

Heisenberg	Bachelard	Jung
Bohr	Gonseth	Adler
De Broglie	Reichenbach	Durkheim
Eddington	Cassirer	Lévy-Bruhl
Dirac	Destouches	Frazer
Hilbert	The Wien School	Von Mises
Weyl	Hayek	
	Robbins	

c) What is living and what is dead in:

Mach	Lamarck
Poincaré	Darwin
Helmholtz	Haeckel
Hertz	Driesch
Riemann	De Vries
Duhem	Freud
Meyerson	Walras
Enriques	Pareto

d) Essays on the classical philosophers and scientists, for example Galileo, Descartes, Leibniz, Newton, Maupertuis, Hamilton, Laplace, etc., always from the point of view of scientific methodology.

Part II. Variety

The journal will also include lighter articles, polemics, etc. For example:

On reading philosophy (dialogue).

Dialogue on finalism.

Apologue on four ways of doing philosophy.

An error by Bergson.

Debate on Geremicca,[33] and those who appreciated him.

Part III. Review

Thorough critical examination of important, recently published works.

Part IV. Criticism

Critical assessments of books should be predominantly informative, with a brief evaluation. An attempt should be made to provide a somewhat complete information, so that the reader is made aware of everything published in Italy and abroad on the issues covered and has a clear view of the contents of each work and its place in current scholarship.

Annex: Letter to Ursula

Melfi, May 10th 1942[34]

Dearest,

I'm writing this letter before I go to bed because I want to answer you immediately about the journal. What you wrote to me has given me a strong desire to work. And you see I was right that it was only there that you would find support and understanding.

---

[33]The complete reference for the quote from Alberto V. Geremicca cited by Colorni is as follows: *Spiritualità nella natura. Istinto, ereditarietà, intelligenze, sviluppo ed evoluzione*, Laterza, Bari, 1938 (note by G. Cerchiai, 2009, p. 76).

[34]Now in Colorni, 2016, p. 84–86.

1) First of all I want to say that I conceive of the journal as having a very definite orientation, that is with a precisely set program and concrete arguments to be developed and advocated. What this orientation will be is difficult to set out in a few words, but it is very clear in my mind, and I'm sure that it fits completely with the concepts I recently read about in the article "Scientific Culture," published in *Philosophical Studies.* Briefly, the idea is to start from a "conventionalist" or "adequatist" conception of science, but rather than limiting it to the philosophical interpretation of scientific facts the way the Vienna School or even Gouseth does, to apply it instead to the basic concepts underlying the edifice of science and show how a rigorous clarification of the hypotheses implicit in the adoption of such concepts can effectively transform and further clarify many scientific formulations, and perhaps resolve some of the knottiest problems modern science faces. A radical challenge, then, to any "realist" or "finalist" position, and also to the facile and equivocal idealist interpretations of the "uncertainty principle" etc. An explicit recognition, rather, of the Kantian origins of such a viewpoint.

2) On this basis I feel we can gain the consensus of everyone who leans in the direction of the Vienna School. As close collaborators I think we can take on Geymonat and Preti, whose article on the subject "what is logic" I found interesting but somewhat confused. We could ask for contributions from the students of Enriques (if there are any) or from Enriques himself. Perhaps we could ask for something from the school of Pastore (which I hardly know, however). The true Italian physicists, almost all students of Fermi, are as far as I know too "realist" to have any concrete interest in a journal of this kind. We might ask some of them (for example, Persico, or Wick) for articles on specific topics that interest us: for example on Eddington's work on the unification of universal constants or on the presuppositions (not the conclusions) of the methodology of Heisenberg For the physics, then, I would think that Geymonat, Preti and I could map out a program of themes to be addressed, developing some of them ourselves, and also asking for specific contributions from experts.

3) For the presentation of the most significant current trends, I think it would be possible to ask the main proponents of these

to present them themselves; with us taking the role of critic. Let me explain: in one issue, for example, there might be an article in which Reichenbach lays out the principles of his thinking; and with it there would be a critique by one of us of Reichenbach's position. It would be even better if Reichenbach's article were his response to a critical essay.

4) For the biology section I find myself very short of ideas and contacts. Bertin it seems to me ought to be able to help with this. For the psychology section I think some help might come from the editors of the *Rivista di Psicologia Sperimentale*. Cantoni could probably inform us concerning research on primitives. For economics, I think we could ask Ernesto and Altiero for help. Ernesto could write an excellent essay on "what is alive and what is dead in Pareto." And an interesting discussion might develop around Robbins's *Essay on the Nature and Significance of Economic Science,* which represents for economics, in my view, what the *Breviario d'Estetica* (Compendium of Aesthetics) was in its day for the science of art.

5) As a general rule, I think the editorial presence in the magazine should be very pronounced. Essays with tendencies different from those of the magazine should be welcomed, but they should be accompanied by comments and arguments from the editors; and all this should display the almost collective nature of the editing and would be better left unsigned.

6) If it looks like the thing is going ahead, gathering of material should begin immediately so that we are ready for the beginning of the coming year with enough material for several issues already in hand. I think the journal should come out punctually every two months, at least.

For this reason, I wouldn't favor starting to bring out anything on "Philosophical studies." We need to keep what we have in reserve, so that we're not short of material when the time comes for the magazine to come out.

Banfi would of course be the ideal director. I think we could look for helpers in his circle of students as well. I had also thought of Giovannino as director for the physics section, but now he is dead. Who will the new professor of theoretical physics in Milan be? But I think once the journal is launched, new contributors will come on their own.

So there it is. I've written this letter in a hurry so I can post it tomorrow, and that way you'll get it in time. Pardon my handwriting and the rushed tone.

A big hug
Your Eugenio

5. "The Strength and Vitality of Love"

A significant example of Colorni's intellectual effervescence, the excerpts "On love" coming from his essays and correspondence expose a real wellspring in Eugenio's extraordinary life, work and action, and reveal the true starting point of his final political exploit.

From the Ventotene Letters to Ursula Hirschmann[35]

May 27th 1939

Pini my dearest,

My new discovery is this: that loving someone means listening to them, understanding even what they don't say, 'translating their words,' and above all not 'shaping' them, not putting them into a frame that you already love and hate from the start. The ever-present danger in a person's life lies in 'identifications' — the transformation of everything into those three or four 'types' that make up the affective mode that we carry with us from childhood. The strength and vitality of love consists, then, in overcoming, breaking these identifications, in 'submitting' to a person and 'listening to them' just as they are, not in doing them violence trying to force them into one of those frames. Note that this advice is directed at me.

June 10th 1939

Dear colleague,[36]

I don't believe most nervous disorders are inherited, but rather 'induced' (the word that seems to fit the case best) by parents who, even in their love for their children, get dragged into these 'identifications' — to satisfy instincts and feelings the children haven't got the slightest idea about: that is, essentially, in loving their children, they think more about themselves than the children. (And I am more and more convinced that true love means letting the loved one 'exist').

---

[35]See also, as a premonition, the Dec. 12th 1938 letter, above.
[36]Ursula had just earned her university degree.

June 12th 1939

My Pini,

Remember that being apart we understand many things: for example why my own wife is so much more intelligent when she is far from me, while I am more intelligent when I am near her: then I can understand what it means to be a spiritual hoarder. And other little things like that.

June 14th 1939

My dearest Pini,

When I behave badly you love me just the same, and you don't think I'm bad, but only that some nastiness has to leave me. That is, when I'm bad you don't think of yourself but of me. And this is what loving means. And I want to tell you something that's been on my mind a lot these days: that when you're here, I would like to let you forget that I'm here too. I don't know if you understand me. I would like you not to feel my cumbersome and clutching presence. I would like to leave you in freedom and solitude, so that you speak and I just shut up and watch you. And you eat bananas at the restaurant: this has always been my theory as well.

From the Conclusions of
"Philosophical Criticism and Theoretical Physics"[37]

Up to the time of Kant, man had made the fundamental laws of the spirit into a sort of safe harbor where he could take refuge when he felt stunned and frightened by the immense diversity of the world. The criterion just like you dominates both Christian and stoic morality, as well as the thinking of the enlightenment. In the depths of his own soul a man believes there is a basis for judging the souls of all other men and, since Kant, judging nature as well. You want to know the world? Look inside yourself: this maxim sums up the great revolution that shifts the method of introspection and self-analysis, so long valid in the field of morality, into the realm of objective knowledge. . . . The essential law of human nature is reason, and reason is also the essential law of the outside

---

[37]Ventotene 1940, now in Colorni, 2009, p. 233–35.

world since man is bound to project outside himself the essence of his own nature. The enormous progress of the natural sciences is explained by the fact that they have placed their own fundamental laws inside the human soul and have thus been reduced, in the last analysis, to the study of man. . . .

With the humanization of the eternal laws of reason and nature thanks to Kant, the enlightenment reached its highest peak. But . . . it also came close to its dissolution. Anything man possesses totally loses all its attraction for him and needs to be dissolved or put behind him. Kant, in presenting man with this great toy — his own powers of reason — also fatally sparked the need to break it to pieces, to be dissatisfied with it and look for something else. If enlightenment is based on what is equal among men, romanticism seeks what is different and unique. And it is no longer reason, but sentiment, character, and passion. It is no longer what we have in common, but what distinguishes us; no longer the universal, but the individual.

In the moral sphere, in the area of relations with other men, this attitude presents itself . . . as an act of humility, a renunciation of anthropomorphism. Man, who believed he had inside himself the criterion for judging other men and nature, has realized that this criterion is insufficient, that it causes him to miss the most interesting and unexpected aspects of his fellow creatures. . . . No longer 'do unto others what you would have them do unto you,' but rather 'do to others what they would have you do to them.' . . . Different, and precisely for that reason difficult to understand, to guess, to discover. It requires an infinite amount of attention to detail, detachment from habits, and love.

Love, whose forms and evolution in the development of modern culture make a fascinating study, is perhaps the spiritual form in which this attitude most typically manifests itself. No longer intended in the medieval sense, as total passion and the annihilation of two beings in one another (Tristan) or a projection onto the beloved of an ideal image (Dolce Stil Novo) or even as the simple satisfying of an instinct; but the way it has been configured in our society — that is, as a complex, sentimental, emotional relationship involving habits and personal interests between two beings who consider themselves moral and spiritual equals — love is perhaps for a modern man the most direct, scorching experience of 'the existence of another person,' a person who is often very different from him in character, likes and dislikes habits and childhood memories. To allow her to exist by his side, indeed to desire her existence more than his own, not trying to absorb her precisely because of her peculiarities, to penetrate that soul with the respect due to a delicate and unknown thing whose balance and harmony might be upset by a rough or abrupt gesture. . . .

From "On Anthropomorphism in the Sciences"[38]
[Commodo-Eugenio Colorni to Severo-Altiero Spinelli]:

We are provided with special organs of attachment, quite different from those that bring scientific knowledge — that predict, that is; but which nevertheless allow us to derive from their use no small amount of satisfaction. . . . They are what I would call organs of loving. By this I mean something truly vast, a generic emotional attitude that includes feelings like hate, friendship, fear, hope, desire, pleasure, pain, etc. It is these organs of attachment that we use on objects that resemble us. And this is for the fundamental reason that in the end they are the same basic organs of attachment that we use on ourselves. . . .

Now, the way of love proceeds along many paths: but if there is one that it is incompatible with and that indeed kills it, it is prediction. Loving in the true and non-degenerate sense of the word means seeing your own object of love as supremely other and therefore always new, always a mystery, every time met with surprise as if for the first time: in a word, unforeseen and alive. And once again this is by analogy with ourselves: because what we love best in ourselves, what we consider most intimately ours, is our freedom of will — the intimate and essential possibility in us that we can be different every time from what would have been predictable. . . .

When we find ourselves in front of something in which we suppose there is a life-centre similar to our own, our mode of attachment is always emotional. . . . And this leads us to think that this emotional mode of attachment is actually the transfer to others

---

[38]Ventotene 1941, now in Colorni, 2009, p. 311–12.

of a feeling that we initially have about ourselves. . . . For this rea-son I don't care much for your description [Severo-Altiero Spinel-li][39] of the two men who want to defeat each other and take turns using each other but are unable to do so because each, in using the other, resists being used himself. Your experience of contact with another man as a collision, a struggle, an effort to overwhelm or be overwhelmed seems to me the worst aspect of everything you do and think. The relationship with another centre of life is for you always somehow a failure of self-assertion. . . .[40]

The means of attachment to a man who doesn't want to allow himself to be used and who in turn wants to use you is, in my view [Colorni], to give up the struggle and let yourself be used. . . . What I mean to say is that the true means of emotional attachment to another man is to let him be, not transform him to suit my ways, but to enjoy his being different from me. . . .[41]

From the Melfi Letters to Ursula Hirschmann

March 1st 1942

My dear,
I've been thinking a lot of things in these times as well. For ex-

---

[39]The essentials of it are in Altiero Spinelli ["Fini e mezzi"] Ventotene 1941; now in E. Colorni and A. Spinelli, 2018, p. 121–34.

[40]The thread of the discussion follows the relationship between being and the need to be. Eugenio cannot deny (obviously) that relations of subjugation exist in politics (Altiero's example is probably one of them) or economics (see, on this point, in "Sul concetto di 'amore,'" the idea of economic man or that resentment can be a tool for gaining access to the realm of freedom. Colorni, 2009, p. 255). The point is that in his view such relations should not dominate the scene between men and women.

[41]"This," Commodo-Eugenio continues, "is what I mean by the love and comprehension of another person. Not 'don't do to others what you don't want done to you,' but 'do to another what he would want done to him.' Not 'to know others look inside yourself,' but 'to know others look at others.' And notice what is theirs, what is peculiar, what is different from you. Don't look for points of contact, least common denominators, universal catego-ries, etc. Try to learn their language without always using yours as a basis of comparison. And so on." As we see, the awareness reacted in this way [utilizing a proposition that originated with Leibniz: see the note of Geri Cerchiai in Colorni, 2009, p. 313] allows Eugenio to 'hook onto' the conclusion of "Philosophical criticism and theoretical physics" (see above). Hence, once again, a particular "way of doing history, seeing it as humanity's past, onto which our own past is grafted, is evidently how, to a very great extent, not predic-tion but affection comes in (in the broad sense discussed earlier)" (Colorni 2009, p. 317).

ample that love is always a state of unstable equilibrium and we're in trouble if it stops being that and turns into a stable one. And that just because it is an unstable equilibrium it is subject to sudden failure. But also that, for this same reason, the worst thing is to keep worrying about maintaining it, preserving it, protecting it. This is what turns it into a stable equilibrium, which means killing it. And so? So the only thing is to have the courage to face the unstable equilibrium, to be ready for anything, never sure about tomorrow. . . . And to calmly imagine that perhaps tomorrow everything might be over.

May 2nd 1942

My own,[42]

It is true that love makes you grow and helps you become 'the world.' But to use love as an opportunity, a way of growing, is precisely what holds you back. In love the big thing is the other, not yourself. . . . I very much want to be loved by you, but not because of my need to be loved; rather because I want to be able to give you that joy and that pain, that swelling of the heart, soul and senses, that Hilflosigkeit [helplessness]. I want to give this to you, I want it to be yours so that it will help you to grow and bloom.

[No date, second half of May 1942]

Dearest,

I have to tell you something that happened just this second that made me happy: I shouted at Silvia because no sooner does somebody come round . . . than she wants to go out with him. I really let her have it and she was utterly humiliated. Then I say: Ok, come and give me a kiss. And she runs over all happy as if nothing had happened. And then I realize that behind her humiliated face there was a smile ready the whole time that had just been waiting for a chance to show itself. And I say: 'But you're not frightened at all when Dad shouts at you!' She looks at me a little bit shamefaced and then says: 'No.' I: 'Why not?' She: 'Well even when you scold me I can see you love me: I understand it now (word for word). I

---

[42]The excerpts from this letter to Ursula is a comment on a fragment taken from *Letters to a Young Poet*, by Rainer Maria Rilke.

see it in your face.' This gave me a real boost.

From "Last Wishes"[43]

I would just urge them [my little ones[44]] to consider love as the most serious and important thing in life; the thing that brings us close to another being, forgetting ourselves and wanting that person to live in their own essence, so very different from us. I would urge them not to squander their feelings, not to mistake superficial and passing excitement for love. These same wishes go to my wife, whom I bless along with our three little ones, hoping with all my heart that she finds the serene happiness that my incapable, unhappy, desperate love was never able to give her.

---

[43]Melfi, May 2nd 1943; now in Colorni, 2017, p. 143.
[44]Silvia, Renata and Eva Colorni.

PART III

1. Unanimity[45]

As a leader of the early European Federalist Movement in Rome, Eugenio wrote this editorial for Unità Europea. Voce del Movimento Federalista Europeo, *n. 2, August 1943, following the fall of Mussolini, in a moment of joy and hope soon to be dashed by the Nazi occupation of Rome. It is a text that is both cautious and firm, navigating between euphoria and anxiety.*

Today the Italian people begin once again to think. They begin thinking at the most difficult moment of their history, with powerful forces threatening them, and it seems as if their fate is being played out in a game they can't follow. They had to fall right to the bottom of the abyss to find the genuineness and self-confidence they had lost. But recriminations are not our aim. The reckoning will come in its own time and place.

What we have seen in these last days has given us a lot to think about. We have joined in unforgettable explosions of joy and enthusiasm on the part of a people almost astonished to find the strength and ability to express themselves. But we have also seen lost and uncertain masses, unaccustomed to freedom, *quaerens cui oboediat* [wondering whom to obey].

From this moment on we want to be perfectly clear: what has happened does not mean simply that the Italian people have changed their government and that this exonerates them from the responsibilities hanging over them. Today we find ourselves faced with elementary and exceptional problems whose solutions cannot be dictated except by the immediate consciousness of the people, even a people just released from servitude. Peace or war? Germany or the United Nations? Fascism or liberty?

We find ourselves at this crossroads in spite of the fall of Mussolini, which has not yet led to the fall of fascism in Europe, or even, entirely, in Italy. We must move beyond this crossroads as

---

[45]Now in Colorni, 2017, p. 175–78.

soon as possible, and there is no appeal to the difficulty of the moment, to the delicacy of the situation, to the diplomatic complexity of the negotiations, that can exempt our leaders from feeling bound by the powerful voice that surges from the Italian people today, crying,

Peace, out with the Nazis, Liberty!

In twenty years of fascism and vaunted "unanimity," there was never any unanimity truer, deeper or more immediately felt than this. And it is a great venture for the Italian people, at the moment when they begin again to be masters of their own destiny, to find themselves united in these aspirations, so simple and yet so decisive for their entire future. Nothing today is more important than these three things; and anyone who thinks they can slow them down even for a single instant so as to preserve established positions or to avoid disorder, commits a true crime of treason against the homeland.

The road to be travelled is long. But along the way there are some obligatory steps, things that must be dealt with right away without a moment's hesitation. This is the task of the present military government. This alone is why it exists, and only if this task is carried out will it have done a great service to Italy and to tomorrow's Europe.

It is not difficult to listen to the voice of the people, which is of course the voice that dominates the conscience of every single Italian. The sooner Italy emerges from the absurd and tragic situation fascism has dragged it into, and the sooner it is able once again to show its true face, the stronger its voice will be and the more encompassing its right to take part in the construction of a free and united Europe.

It is not just today that we say these things. Our movement, born under the most ferocious fascist oppression, knows the hard life of illegality and conspiracy. Its people have long been accustomed to prisons and islands of confinement. If today we ask for the right to come out into the light of day, it is because we know that we are carrying our people's most deeply felt message and signalling the goal that, on pain of death, we must achieve.

A Parallel

The 1919 Treaty of Versailles left a Europe composed of 35 sovereign states the in place of the 25 that had existed at the outbreak of the war, and consequently with an additional 11,000 kilometers of additional customs barriers. This fact alone makes it clear that the new European structure could not have come out less unstable than the previous one. The restrictive economic measures adopted by each state toward each of the others were progressively tightened to the point that the different sovereign nations had become so many watertight compartments. This inflexibility led to the adoption of the most absurd restrictions — monetary, commercial, migratory and even concerning tourism. Divided in this way, weighed down by enormous military expenditures and enmeshed in a web of restrictions of every kind, Europe could never have reached a level of prosperity comparable to that of the United States of America. This parallel is extremely significant. The United States constitutes a political-economic region with a surface area greater than that of all the European countries combined, excluding Russia (7,839,000 vs 5,275,000 sq. kms.). The unified market, with a correspondingly more rational division of labor under different environmental conditions has made labor in the United States vastly more productive than in Europe, which explains the higher standard of living of Americans with respect to Europeans.

What would conditions be like for these same Americans, on the other hand, if each of today's federal states constituted a market in itself, one that tended toward autocracy in the interests of greater security and was forced as a result into heavy peacetime military spending and periodic bloody wars over supremacy or disputed borders or some other issue? The Federation of 48 American republics is the fundamental reason for the extraordinary well-being of the United States and its citizens.

2. The Socialists and the European Federation[46]

Through this declaration of principles, Eugenio's federalism came to the fore among socialists, eventually becoming a point of reference, especially for young generations of antifascists.

Italian socialists want the peace that follows this war to lay the foundations of a solid united organization established in a Federation of Free European States. This entails the rejection of any League of Nations project which leaves the economic, political and military structure of the various states intact and offers a mere super-state in which single countries are represented with their full sovereignty undiminished, and against whose decisions any state or group of states with sufficient strength can remain recalcitrant. The only premise that precludes the possibility that political, economic or social achievements can suddenly be overturned by another imperialist war is the formation of a single European Federation with representative institutions whose members the citizens elect directly and not through the various states, a Federation that will provide a single market through a rationalized economic organization, with a working of its own, leaving to the individual states only the maintenance of domestic order. Such a Federation, while safeguarding national cultural and linguistic autonomy, will provide for the deep and intimate contact between peoples that should give rise to a renewed European consciousness.

Italian socialists believe that this prospect, one that might still have seemed a distant ideal only a few years ago, will prove to be very close to fulfillment in the period following the present war, and are furthermore convinced that such a goal is closely linked to the objectives they pursue as socialists, given that the formation of a unifying European Federation is an event of such revolutionary importance that it cannot happen without the active participation

---

[46]Now in Colorni, 2017, p. 183–84.

of the masses in a thorough and general social renewal of our continent. For Italy, as for all the populations who emerge as losers from this war, such a solution would also be the only way to avoid defeat, territorial mutilation and economic subjugation.

The Italian Socialist Party believes that it is specifically the attitude of the masses that will make the crucial difference in this regard. It will create situations on the ground that the winners will be forced to take into account, prompting action and pushing the international situation in the direction of European Unity.

3. "Preface" to Problems of the European Federation[47]

Eugenio Colorni's "Preface" to Problems of the European Federation *by Altiero Spinelli and Ernesto Rossi (a booklet published in Rome on January 22nd, 1944, that contains the Ventotene "Manifesto") is a small masterpiece in itself. Distributed clandestinely in Rome, it eloquently supported the quest for a European federation that Colorni considered a major achievement of his time in political advocacy. He suggested it as a pole star for daily struggles as well as a useful pedagogic tool, especially for young generations of anti-fascists.*

The present writings were conceived and drafted on the island of Ventotene in the years 1941 and 1942. In that unusual environment, under conditions of the most rigid discipline and the unhappiness of enforced inertia along with an eagerness for imminent liberation, and based on information which a thousand precautions had rendered as complete as possible, a process of rethinking began in several minds concerning all the issues that had motivated the actions and positions taken in the struggle.[48]

The isolation from concrete political activity allowed for a more detached view and suggested a review of traditional positions and a search for the reasons for past failures, not so much in technical errors of parliamentary or revolutionary tactics or in a generic "immaturity" of the situation, as in deficiencies in the general approach and in having committed the struggle to the usual fault lines, paying too little attention to what was new and was altering the situation.

In preparation for efficiently fighting the great battle for the near future that was looming, we felt a need not simply to correct the errors of the past, but to reformulate the terms of the political

---

[47]Now in Colorni, 2107, p. 193–99.

[48]This text is certainly attributable to the pen of Eugenio Colorni. It was published in a volume edited by Colorni himself that appeared in January 1944 under the title *Problemi della federazione europea,* which contained, along with the "Manifesto," two other documents drawn up by Altiero Spinelli [note by Leo Solari]

issues with minds unencumbered by doctrinaire preconceptions or party myths.

Thus it was that in the minds of certain people[49] the key idea took shape that the basic contradiction responsible for the crises, wars, misery and exploitation afflicting our society was the existence of sovereign states that are geographically, economically and militarily defined, which view other states as competitors and potential enemies, and live in a perpetual state of *bellum omnium contra omnes* with respect to each other.

There are many reasons why this idea, although not new in itself, took on a new significance on the occasion and under the conditions in which it was conceived [that is, on Ventotene at the beginning of the 1940s]:

1) First of all, the internationalist solution, which appears on the agendas of all progressive political parties, is in a certain sense considered by each of them to be a necessary and almost automatic consequence of achieving the ends that each of these parties proposes. The democrats maintain that the establishment within each country of the regime they advocate will surely lead to the formation of that unitary consciousness which, passing beyond all cultural and moral frontiers, will constitute the basis, for them indispensable, of a free union of peoples, even in the areas of politics and economics. And the socialists, for their part, think that the establishment of the dictatorship of the proletariat in the various states will in itself lead to an international collectivist state.

Now, an analysis of the modern concept of the state and the interests and feelings linked to it[50] clearly shows that although sim-

---

[49]"In the first half of 1939," Altiero Spinelli recalled (1985, p. 201–02), "reading articles that Einaudi had published at the end of 1918 in the *Corriere della Sera* against the League of Nations in favor of a European federation, reading certain essays by English federalist authors, reading Meinecke's book *Nationalstaat und Staatrason* . . . as well as reflecting on Europe's apparent march towards a new World War, I began to think that probably, the future of Europe, once fascism and Nazism fall, would have to be sought not simply in the restoration of national democracies but in the establishment of a European federation. . . . This idea was first born in my discussions with Rossi. . . . When we began talking about this idea with others, Eugenio and his wife Ursula were among the first to embrace it."

[50]This reference to interests and sentiments clearly recalls to us *The Passions and the Interests,* by Albert Hirschman (1977). Further, it implicitly reveals Eugenio's concern for the need to reconcile the interests and sentiments of different countries in a federalist arrangement.

ilarities in internal regimes can facilitate friendly relations and collaboration between one state and another, it is by no means certain that this will automatically or even progressively lead to unification, as long as there are collective interests and feelings associated with maintaining a unity confined within borders. We know from experience that chauvinistic feelings and protectionist interests can easily lead to clash and competition even between two democracies; there is nothing to say that a rich socialist state would necessarily pool its own resources with another much poorer socialist state merely because it was governed by a similar regime.

The abolition of political and economic borders between States, therefore, does not necessarily derive from the simultaneous establishment of a given internal regime in each state; it is an issue in its own right, and must be tackled using appropriate means tailored specifically to it. It is true that it is not possible to be socialists without also being internationalists; but this is due to an ideological connection rather than political and economic necessity, and a socialist victory in individual states does not necessarily lead to an international state.

2) What also urged us to give prominence autonomously to the federalist proposal was the fact that existing political parties, tied to a history of struggles fought within the confines of each nation, are by habit and tradition accustomed to defining all problems on the tacit assumption of the existence of the nation-state and considering problems at the international level as issues of 'foreign policy' to be resolved through diplomacy and agreements between various governments. This point of view is partly the cause and partly the consequence of the attitude mentioned above whereby, once power has been seized in one's own country, agreement and union with similar regimes in other countries will automatically come about without the need for a political struggle expressly dedicated to this end.

The authors of the present writings, on the other hand, held the deep-rooted conviction that anyone who wished to pose the problem of the international order as central to the current historical era and treat its solution as a necessary prerequisite to solving all our society's institutional, economic and social problems, would have to extend this point of view to all issues concerning internal political contrasts and the attitude of each party, even regarding the tactics and strategy of the daily struggle. All issues, from constitutional liberty to class struggle, from planning to gaining power and using it, take on a new light when articulated starting from the premise that the primary goal is a united international system.[51] Even political maneuvering — aligning oneself with one or another of the forces at play, highlighting one catchphrase or another — takes on a very different significance depending on whether the essential aim is to seize power and implement certain reforms within the ambit of each single state, or to create the economic, political and moral prerequisites for the establishment of a federal order that embraces the entire continent.

3) Yet another reason — perhaps the most important — is the fact that while the ideal of a European federation, the precursor to a global federation, may have seemed a distant utopia until a few years ago, it now appears, at the end of this war, to be an achievable goal and almost within reach. The complete reshuffling of populations that this conflict has provoked in all the countries under German occupation; the need to reconstruct on new foundations an economy that has been almost completely destroyed and to refocus attention on all the problems concerning political boundaries, customs barriers, ethnic minorities, etc.; the very character of this war, in which the national element has so often been overshadowed by the ideological element, in which small and medium-sized states have surrendered much of their sovereignty to stronger states; and in which the fascists themselves have replaced the concept of 'national independence' with that of 'living space': all these elements should be recognized as evidence that the federal ordering of Europe is more topical than ever before.

Forces from all social classes, for reasons that are both economic and idealistic, may be interested in it. It can be approached

---

[51]Amazing, in this regard, is the consonance with what Albert Hirschman was then writing on the other side of the world in California (1942, published in 1945) and that later (1978) he would consider "infinitely naïve" (up to a certain point — one may suggest). (Meldolesi, 2013, Ch. 3 and 1994, Ch. 4.)

by means of diplomatic negotiation and popular agitation, and by promoting the study of problems related to the issue among the educated classes, provoking *de facto* conditions of revolution from which it will be impossible to turn back; we can do this by influencing the upper echelons of the victorious states and spreading the word in defeated states that only in a free and united Europe will they be able to find salvation and avoid the disastrous consequences of defeat.

The reason our Movement arose is precisely this. It is the preeminence, the precedence of this problem over all the others that afflict us in the period we are now going through; it is the sure knowledge that if we let the situation re-solidify in the old nationalistic molds, the opportunity will be lost forever, and our continent will have no lasting peace and well being. All of this is what motivated us to create an autonomous organization whose purpose is to champion the idea of the European Federation as an achievable goal in the post-war period.

We do not hide the difficulties of this, nor the power of the forces ranged on the other side; but it is the first time, we believe, that this problem has been placed on the table of the political struggle not as a distant ideal, but as a pressing, tragic necessity.

Our Movement has for approximately two years now lived a difficult clandestine life under fascist and Nazi oppression. Its adherents come from the militant ranks of anti-fascism and are all in the front line of the armed struggle for freedom. It has paid a hard price in prison for the common cause. It is a Movement that is not and does not want to be a political party. Its character has become increasingly clear: the Movement aims to work with and within the various political parties, not only to bring the internationalist issue to the foreground, but also — mainly — to ensure that all the political problems related to the issue are framed from the perspective of this new visual angle, to which the parties have until now been so little accustomed.

We are not a political party because, while actively promoting every manner of study concerning the institutional, economic and social structure of the European Federation, taking an active part in the struggle to bring it into being and concerning ourselves to discover what forces might act in its favor in the future political situation, we do not want to take an official position concerning the institutional details, the level of economic collectivization, the degree of administrative decentralization, etc., etc., that ought to characterize this future federal body. Suffice it to say that in the bosom of our Movement these problems are widely and freely discussed and that every political tendency, from communist to liberal, is represented among us. Indeed, almost all our adherents carry weight in one or another of the progressive political parties and all agree in supporting the basic principles of a free European Federation that is not based on any kind of hegemony or totalitarian order, and is endowed with a structural solidity that does not reduce it to a simple League of Nations.

These principles may be summarized as follows: a single federal army, a single currency, abolition of customs barriers and emigration limits among the Federation's member states, direct representation of citizens in federal assemblies, and a unified foreign policy.

In its two years of life our Movement has spread widely among anti-fascist groups and political parties. Some of them have publicly expressed their adherence and their sympathy. Others have called on us to collaborate on their policy statements. It would perhaps not be presumptuous to say that it is partly to our credit that the problems of the European Federation are so often discussed in the Italian underground press. Our journal, *L'Unità Europea*, closely follows domestic and international events, taking positions on them with absolute independence of judgment.

The present writings, the result of the development of the ideas that led to the birth of our Movement, represent nothing more than the opinion of the authors and do not in any way constitute the position of the Movement itself. They are intended only as a proposal of topics for discussion for anyone who wants to rethink the problems of international political life in the light of the most recent ideological and political experiences, the most up-to-date findings of economics, and the most sensible and reasonable prospects for the future.

They will be followed presently by other studies. Our hope is that they will stimulate an outpouring of ideas, and that in the present atmosphere, alive with the urgent need for action, they will provide the clarity that will make such action ever more resolute, clear-eyed and responsible.

The Italian Movement for a European Federation
Rome, 22 January 1944

4. Administration and Revolution

Taken together, the excerpts from two articles — "Administration or revolution" and "Revolution from above?"-, published a brief distance apart by the clandestine Avanti!, respectively on n. 15 and 18 in May 1944,[52] exemplify Eugenio's political thought and perspective on the verge of the liberation of Rome.

Administration or Revolution

There are those who believe that the essential purpose of taking power is to do as little harm as possible while guiding the country out of the tragic difficulties the fascist war plunged it into; to eliminate this failed legacy in such a way that people suffer as little as possible; to administer the state so that it settles gradually into shape; to earn merit in the eyes of the victorious powers. Worthwhile tasks, without doubt, that no responsible party, least of all ours, would back away from. But this sort of limited vision entails viewing the future of Europe and the world from a series of perspectives that we do not hesitate to call reactionary. It entails first of all the view that at the end of this war everything will remain as before internationally, except for a few shifting frontiers and modifications in power relations between various countries; it entails believing that nations' sovereignty and independence will remain intact, except for a few sanctions the victors will want to impose; it entails interpreting today's frequently heard expressions referring to peoples' 'independence' and 'self-determination' in the most small-minded and archaic way — in the sense, that is, that each country will have to go on as a unit in itself from a political, economic and military point of view, and will look after its own reconstruction essentially employing its own internal resources behind the protection of its customs barriers, if need be accepting the support of other powers in the form of diplomacy or financial credit.

---

[52]Now in Colorni, 2017, p. 201–04 and 205–07.

Anyone who comes forward to contend for power on the basis of this view cannot help but view the job as one of ordinary — or even extraordinary, let's say — administration. The purpose is a return to 'normalcy', which essentially means the status quo ante. Take the country back to where it was before the beginning of the tragic adventure that ended so disastrously; from there, take up the struggle again, maybe with more daring ideas this time, taking care not to fall into the errors of the past.

With a greater or lesser degree of conscious awareness, many view the problem of power in these terms. But they do not comprehend the enormity of the crisis that engulfs us. They do not realize that we are moving into a pre-eminently revolutionary era at the international level; and that it is only by participating decisively in this great movement that we can hope to make a conclusive contribution to the well-being of our country and the progress of humanity. The crisis that will soon erupt with the collapse of Germany and will surely strike the Balkan countries, probably along with Scandinavia and France, may well take on the aspect of a great European revolution in which the entire political, economic and social orientation of our continent is called into question. All institutional problems will be re-formulated from this perspective; all social reforms will take on a new meaning in this framework. It will not do to object that the winners alone will decide the essentials of Europe's new orientation, and that all that remains for the people on the losing side is to work within the imposed framework. Starting now, in all the countries subjected to German occupation, revolutionary movements are in action that will certainly not respond to the problems of reconstruction as passive bystanders; starting now, even in England and America (not to speak of Russia), progressive forces are in motion, putting forward non-imperialist solutions aimed at eliminating once and for all the danger of repeated warfare through a total renewal of the European economic and social structure on a unified basis.

The purpose of a progressive party that intends to win power in its country is to ready itself and ready the people for this great event; to establish the foundations for the active participation of the entire nation in this total renewal of the very basis of our social coexistence; to be an actor, not a spectator or, worse yet, a blind follower in the decisive events we are about to face.

Revolution from Above?

It may be that we have seen the end of the era of great mass movements crucial to the future life of a people, the romantic era of revolution as a people's rising in which fluctuations in popular favor are decisive for the life of a nation. Today, the scope of the game has widened, and the ties of interdependence between a country's internal regime and the general political framework have multiplied. Every shift in balance even in a peripheral area has repercussions at the centre, so that world political leaders can no longer consider the will of the people in any country as an autonomous fact with its own developmental trajectory, but must view it as an element in an extremely complex game in which all the strings must be kept firmly under control.

Must we conclude from all this that if there is a revolution, it will be a revolution from above, brought about or even imposed by the winners? Must we gloomily resign ourselves to no longer having anything to say about our destiny, to being almost pawns in a game whose course we cannot influence? Must we limit our activity to going along with the plans of whichever winning power we are aligned with, taking its every policy maneuver as a directive we simply have to get used to?

We do not believe this for a second. We believe that opposition to this tendency is one of the essential reasons for our party's existence. In assessing the function of mass movements and the free expression of popular will in the present situation, we must consider the fact that these same winning powers have not yet begun to decide what political line they will follow with respect to postwar problems. Their opinions are far from unequivocal, and even in their own minds they have conflicting tendencies. . . .

It is into this still uncertain and fluctuating context, in the current delicate political moment, that mass actions must decisively move. Their purpose is to influence public opinion, chancellors' offices, military headquarters: to show what can be done and what cannot be done. A clear "no" from the people and from the parties that represent them can today be decisive in causing the re-evaluation of a situation and radical changes of attitude in the ruling circles of the countries that hold our destiny in their hands.

5. Tribute to Lopresti[53]

This memorial article for Giuseppe Lopresti was published in Avanti!
*of 19 August 1944, after the death of Eugenio Colorni. It represents
his last message.*

There are words that we hesitate to apply to Giuseppe Lopresti
only because they are too commonly used in the pitying rhetoric
of obituaries. He was truly — and not only today, after his martyr-
dom — the best, the most serious, the most sensible, the most pro-
foundly pure of our youth. He was 25 years old. He held a degree
in law and was in his second year of philosophy; he was intelligent
and open to any cultural issue, and with his passionate interest in
religious questions as well, it seemed that all roads were open to
him.

He approached us with extreme naturalness, as if we were a
group he had long been a part of. We felt no hint in him of the distance or detachment that might have come from his having grown
up in a fascist climate. Thanks to him we began to appreciate and
love this wonderful new generation that now fights alongside us
and that seems to have slipped as if by magic through twenty years
of fascism without being soiled by it; bringing on the contrary a
deeper need to live life consciously and intensely. Beppe brought
us close to this youthful world to which we are now so irrevocably
bound; this world of which he was in many ways the spokesperson
and symbol.

He immediately distinguished himself in our military organization as one of the most reliable and efficient elements. He was
entrusted with extremely delicate assignments. Even though he
was young and had only been in contact with us for a short time,
he was one of our leaders. And he undertook these difficult and
risky jobs with utter tranquility, without the slightest presumption,
with that modest cheerfulness so common in strong people, peo-

---

[53]Now in Colorni, 2017, p. 209–10.

ple with a clear conscience. For him, the duty to sacrifice himself and to give his own life was something obvious, not even worth talking about. And he showed it under Nazi torture, taking all responsibility on himself.

I saw him only a few minutes before his arrest; he was concerned about a worsening situation, intent on doing whatever was necessary to save what could still be saved. I will never forget his alert and thoughtful face, already holding a premonition of the death that lay in wait.

The fascists enjoy their inhuman vengeance, but there is one thing they will never know, because they lack the moral standing to understand it: and that is what human values, what spiritual riches they deprive us of with their blind violence. But this, the reason for our terrible pain, is also the source of our fiercest pride.

BIBLIOGRAPHY

AA. VV. (Various Authors) (1963) *Documenti inediti dell'archivio Angelo Tasca. La rinascita del socialismo italiano e la lotta contro il fascismo dal 1934 al 1939 (Unpublished Documents from Angelo Tasca Archive. The Re-Birth of the Italian Socialism and the Struggle against Fascism from 1934 to 1939)*, Stefano Merli ed., Milano Feltrinelli.

____. (2004) *Eugenio Colorni 1944–2004. Dalla guerra alla Costituzione europea [Eugenio Colorni 1944–2004. From the War to the European Constitution]*. Ed. Maria Pia Bumbaca. Roma: Municipio III.

____. (2010) *Eugenio Colorni dall'antifascismo all'europeismo socialista e federalista [Eugenio Colorni from Anti-Fascism to Socialist and Federalist Europeanism]*. Ed. Maurizio degl'Innocenti. Manduria: Lacaita.

____. (2011) *Eugenio Colorni e la cultura italiana tra le due guerre [Eugenio Colorni and the Italian Culture in between the Two Wars]*. Ed. Geri Cerchiai and Giovanni Rota. Manduria: Lacaita.

Adelman, J. (2013) *Wordly Philosopher: The Odyssey of Albert O. Hirschman*. Princeton, NJ: Princeton UP.

Alighieri, D. (1995) *La Divina Commedia [The Divine Comedy]*. London: Everyman Library.

Bobbio, N. (1975) "Introduzione" ["Introduction"]. *Writings*, by Colorni E. Scritti. Ed. Norberto Bobbio. Firenze: La Nuova Italia.

Cerchiai, G. (2009) "Introduzione" ["Introduction"] and "Note ai testi" ["Note to Texts"]. *La malattia della metafisica. Scritti filosofici e autobiografici [The Illness of Metaphysics. Philosophical and Biographical Writings]*, by E. Colorni. Ed. Geri Cerchiai. Torino: Einaudi.

Cervantes, M. de. (2003) *El Ingenioso Hidalgo Don Quixote de la Mancha [The Ingenious Nobleman Mr. Quixote de la Mancha]*. New York: Penguin.

Colorni, E. (1937) "Le verità eterne in Descartes e Leibnitz" ["Eternal Truths in Descartes and Leibnitz"]. *La malattia della metafisica. Scritti filosofici e autobiografici [The Illness of Metaphysics. Philosophical and Biographical Writings]*, by E. Colorni. Ed. Geri Cerchiai. Torino: Einaudi.

____. (1939) "Apologo su quattro modi di filosofare" ["Apologue on Four Ways of Philosophising"]. *La malattia della metafisica. Scritti filosofici e autobiografici [The Illness of Metaphysics. Philosophical and Biographical Writings]*, by E. Colorni. Ed. Geri Cerchiai. Torino. Einaudi.

____. (1940) "Sul concetto di 'amore'" ["On the Concept of 'Love'"]. *La malattia della metafisica. Scritti filosofici e autobiografici [The Illness of Metaphysics. Philosophical and Biographical Writings]*, by E. Colorni. Ed. Geri Cerchiai. Torino: Einaudi.

____. (1981) "Prefazione." *Problemi della Federazione europea [Problems of the European Federation]*, by A. Spinelli and E. Rossi. Ed. Eugenio Colorni. Roma: 1944; English trans. *The Manifesto of Ventotene*, by A. Spinelli and E. Rossi. Rome: Associazione Italiana per il Consiglio dei Comuni d'Europa (AICCE), the Centro Italiano di Formazione Europea (CIFE), and the Movimento Federalista Europe (MFE), Provincia di Latina.

___. (1975) *Scritti* [*Writings*]. Ed. Norberto Bobbio. Firenze: La Nuova Italia.

___. (1988) *Il coraggio dell'innocenza* [*The Courage of Innocence*]. Ed. Luca Meldolesi. Napoli: La Città del Sole.

___. (2009) *La malattia della metafisica. Scritti filosofici e autobiografici* [*The Illness of Metaphysics. Philosophical and Biographical Writings*]. Ed. Geri Cerchiai. Torino: Einaudi.

___. (2016) *Microfondamenta* [*Microfoundations*]. Ed. Luca Meldolesi. Soveria Mannelli: Rubbettino.

___. (2017) *La scoperta del possibile: scritti politici* [*The Discovery of the Possible: Political Writings*]. Ed. Luca Meldolesi. Soveria Mannelli: Rubbettino.

___. (2018) *L'ultimo anno: 1943–1944. Genesi di una prospettiva* [*The Last Year 1943–1944. Genesis of a Political Perspective*]. Ed. Luca Meldolesi. Soveria Mannelli: Rubbettino.

___, and Curiel E. (2005) *Il sogno di una nuova Italia* [*The Dream of a New Italy*]. Ed. Mario Quaranta. Padova: Sapere.

___, and Spinelli A. (2018) *I dialoghi di Ventotene* [*The Ventotene Dialogues*]. Ed. Luca Meldolesi. Soveria Mannelli: Rubbettino.

Croce, B. (1921) *Il breviario di estetica* [*The Essence of Aestetics*]. London: Heineman.

De Sanctis, F. (1912) *Storia della letteratura italiana* [*History of Italian Literature*]. Bari: Laterza.

Einaudi, L. (Junius). (1929) *Lettere politiche* [*Political Letters*]. Bari: Laterza, now in Luigi Einaudi and *Corriere della Sera*. Milano: Fondazione Corriere della Sera (2009).

Enriquez F. (1937) *Il problema della vita* [*The Problem of Life*]. Bologna: Zanichelli.

Foscolo, U. (1966) "Dei sepolcri" ["Sepulchres"]. *Opere* [*Works*]. Ed. Mario Puppo. Milano: Mursia.

Gerbi, S. (1999) *Tempi di malafede. Una storia italiana tra fascismo e dopoguerra. Guido Piovene ed Eugenio Colorni* [*Time of Bad Faith. An Italian Story in between Fascism and Post-War. Guido Piovene and Eugenio Colorni*]. Torino: Einaudi.

Geremicca, A.V. (1939) *Spiritualità nella natura. Istinto, ereditarietà, intelligenza, sviluppo, evoluzione* [*Spirituality in Nature. Instinct, Legacy, Cleverness, Development, Evolution*]. Bari: Laterza.

Goethe, J. W. (1912) *Faust*. 1808–32. London: Dent.

Gui, F. (2010) "Colorni 'elemento di contestazione e di cerniera' nei documenti dell'Archivio centrale dello stato" ["Colorni as 'element of contrast and linkage' in the Dcuments of the Cenral Archives of the State"]. *Eugenio Colorni dall'antifascismo all'europeismo socialista e federalista* [*Eugenio Colorni from Anti-Fascism to Socialist and Federalist Europeanism*]. Ed. Maurizio degl'Innocenti. Manduria: Lacaita.

Hirschman, A. O. (1980) *National Power and the Structure of Foreign Trade*. (first edition 1945) Berkeley, CA: U of California P; third ed., with a new Introduction.

___. (1971) *A Bias for Hope. Essays on Development and Latin America*. New Haven, CT: Yale UP.

___. (1977) *The Passions and the Interests. Political Arguments for Capitalism before Its Triumph*. Princeton, NJ: Princeton UP.

___. (1995) *A Propensity to Self-Subversion*. (first edition 1987). Cambridge, MA: Harvard UP.

Leibnitz, G. G. (1934) *Monadologia* [*Monadology*]. Ed. Eugenio Colorni. Firenze: Sansoni.

Meinecke, F. (1908) *Weltburgertum und Nationalstaat* [*Cosmopolitanism and the National State*]. Vols. 1–2. München: R. Oldenburg.

___. (1924) *Die Idee der Staatsrason in der neuren Geschichte* [*The Idea of Reason of State in Modern History*]. München: R. Oldenburgm.

Meldolesi, L. (1994) *Alla scoperta del possibile. Il mondo sorprendente di Albert O. Hirschman* [*Discovering the Possible. The Suprising World of Albert O. Hirschman*]. Bologna: il Mulino. English translation: Notre Dame: U of Notre Dame P, 1995. Spanish translation: Méxicc: Fondo de Cultura Econòmica, 1997.

___. (2013) *Imparare ad imparare. Saggi di incontro e di passione all'origine di una possibile metamorfosi* [*Learning to Learn. Essays on Encounters and Passions at the Origin of a Possible Metamorphosis*]. Soveria Mannelli: Rubbettino.

___. (2017) "Introduzione. Attualità politica di Eugenio Colorni" ["Introduction. Political actuality of Eugentio Colorni"]. Colorni, *La scoperta del possibile. Scritti politici.*

Nietzsche F. W. (2003) *Jenseits von Gut und Bose* [*Beyond Good and Evil*]. New York: Penguin.

Perucca, E. (1937) *Fisica generale e sperimentale* [*General and Experimental Physics*]. Torino: Utet.

Petrarca, F. (2002) *Canzoniere* [*Song Book*]. 1374. New York: Penguin.

Quaranta, M. (2011) "La 'scoperta' di Eugenio Colorni nelle riviste del secondo dopoguerra. Gli scritti sulla relatività" ("The 'Discovery' of Eugenio Colorni in the Second Post-war Journals. Writings on Relativity"). AA. VV., (2011).

Rilke, R. M. (2002) *Briefe an einen jungen Dichter* [*Letters to a Young Poet*]. Dover: Dover.

Robbins, L. (1932) *An Essay on the Nature and Significance of Economic Science.* London: Macmillan.

___. (1937) *Economic Planning and International Order.* London: Macmillan.

___. (1940) *The Economic Causes of the War.* New York: Macmillan.

Rognoni Vercelli, C. (1991) *Mario Alberto Rollier un valdese federalista* [*Mario Alberto Rollier, a Waldensian Federalist*]. Milano: Jaca.

Rossi, E. and A. Spinelli. (1944) *Problemi ella Federazione europea* [*Problems of the European Federation*]. Ed. Eugenio Colorni. Roma.

___. (1981) *The Manifesto of Ventotene,* based on the Colorni edition, published in Rome, by Associazione Italiana per il Consiglio dei Comuni d'Europa (AICCE), the Centro Italiano di Formazione Europea (CIFE) and the Movimento Federalista Europe (MFE), Provincia di Latina.

Simmel, G. (1990) *Philosophie des Geldes* [*Philosophy of Money*]. London: Routledge.

Solari, L. (1980) *Eugenio Colorni. Ieri e sempre* [*Eugenio Colorni. Yesterday and Always*]. Venezia: Marsilio.

Spinelli A. (2018) "Fini e mezzi" ["Ends and Means"]. *Ventotene* 1941. *I dialoghi di Ventotene* [*The Ventotene Dialogues*], by E. Colorni and A. Spinelli. Ed. Luca Meldolesi. Soveria Mannelli: Rubbettino.

___. (1984) *Come ho tentato di diventare saggio. Io, Ulisse* [*How I Tried to Become Wise. I Ulysses*]. Bologna: Il Mulino.

___. (1985) *Il progetto europeo* [*The European Project*]. Bologna: Il Mulino.

___. (1993) *Machiavelli nel secolo XX. Scritti del confino e della clandestinità* [*Machiavelli in the XX Century. Writings from Internment and Underground*]. Ed. Piero Graglia. Bologna: Il Mulino.

___, and E. Colorni. (2018) *I dialoghi di Ventotene* [*The Ventotene Dialogues*]. Ed. Luca Meldolesi. Soveria Mannelli: Rubbettino.

___, and E. Rossi. (1944) *Problemi ella Federazione europea* [*Problems of the European Federation*]. Ed. Eugenio Colorni. Roma.

___. (1981) *The Manifesto of Ventotene*, based on the Colorni edition, published in Rome, by Associazione Italiana per il Consiglio dei Comuni d'Europa (AICCE), the Centro Italiano di Formazione Europea (CIFE) and the Movimento Federalista Europe (MFE), Provincia di Latina.

Voltaire (François Marie Arouet). (1991) *Candide, ou l'Optimisme* [*Candide, or Optimism*]. Dover: Dover.

INDEX OF SUBJECTS

Index of Names